WRITING A DISSERTATION

The Essential Guide

Suzi Richer

Writing a Dissertation: The Essential Guide is also available in accessible formats for people with any degree of visual impairment. The large print edition and e-book (with accessibility features enabled) are available from Need2Know. Please let us know if there are any special features you require and we will do our best to accommodate your needs.

First published in Great Britain in 2013 by
Need2Know
Remus House
Coltsfoot Drive
Peterborough
PE2 9BF
Telephone 01733 898103
Fax 01733 313524
www.need2knowbooks.co.uk

Contents

Introduction

A dissertation is a long piece of original research that is undertaken as part of an undergraduate degree. It is usually started at the end of the second year and is submitted for marking at some point in the third year. Almost every undergraduate student will research and write a dissertation. A dissertation is the chance to put the learning from the previous years into practice and to research a topic that you enjoy learning about. It is the centrepiece of your degree.

Despite a drop in the number of people enrolling in university degrees, *The Guardian* reported in January 2012, that of an overall drop in students of 8.7%, the number of students coming straight from school only dropped by 3.7% – this group is by far the majority of the student body. A university education is still important to people and will continue to be so. There are still more students wishing to go to university than there are places available for them. A significant part of a university education is writing a dissertation.

It might be commonplace to have to write a dissertation, but this shouldn't trivialise the process. Writing a dissertation can be a wonderful experience, where you have the freedom to research something that interests *you*, where *your* ideas are at the heart of the writing and where *you* are in control of *your own* timetable. Equally, it can be an extremely stressful situation; it can be frustrating, lonely and exhausting.

Are you at a loss as to which subject your dissertation should focus on? Are you having problems finding the right supervisor? Do you have the constant worry that you will never finish the research? Have you had problems with your grammar before and are you worried it will let you down now? Do you think that you've left it too late and there isn't a chance of finishing it on time? Do you worry about how your work will compare to your classmates'? If you have any of these worries, you can rest assured that you are not the only one and there are ways around them.

'A significant part of a university education is writing a dissertation.'

'Whether you are just about to start, or whether you have one month left until the deadline and little to show for it, this book is for you.'

This book is written for anyone tackling a dissertation for the first time, in particular undergraduate students. It examines some of the main areas a dissertation needs to cover, but it also addresses some of the key issues you will face along the way. Whether you are just about to start, or whether you have one month left until the deadline and little to show for it, this book is for you. It's filled with hints and tips to help get you through the dissertation as painlessly as possible, therefore helping you to achieve the best mark. This book covers what a dissertation is, how to choose a topic, how to plan your workload, how to structure your dissertation and what the research process involves. The second half of the book will guide you through the writing-up process, helping your grammar and style, assisting you to untangle your results, making sure you look after yourself (both physically and mentally) during the final phase and the submission process. Although you shouldn't need it, there is also a chapter on what to focus on if you feel like you've left everything too late or that you're just running out of time.

Importantly, although the book is written with the student in mind, it should also help parents, friends or relatives supporting someone through writing a dissertation. Having an understanding of what is involved, when the tricky times are likely to occur and what the common problems are, will provide you with some guidance on how best to provide support.

The overall focus of the book is about helping you to stay in control of your dissertation, without letting it dominate your life. During the last week, it may well feel as if it is in control of you, but by having a good plan that you've been working towards and that you continue to work to, you should always be in control of it – even if it doesn't seem like it. This book will act as a handbook for you as you go along, helping you to keep control of the dissertation and at the same time giving you the best opportunity to achieve the mark you deserve.

Note about software

Where a description occurs for how to carry out a task in Microsoft Word, it should be noted that Word 2010 has been used, unless stated otherwise.

Acknowledgements

The experience of many people has gone into writing this book. In particular, I would like to thank the following people for sharing ideas with me, allowing me to quote them or to include examples of their work: Dr Steve Ashby, University of York; Dr Emma Waterton, University of Western Sydney; Dr Kevin Walsh, University of York; Dr Cath Neal, University of York; Robin Wilson, PhD student; Dr Hayley Saul, Head of the Himalayan Exploration Archaeological Research Team; Dr Mari Whitelaw; Mike Sowden, Storytelling consultant; Nick Trustram Eve, founder of The Copper Pot. I would also like to thank Nick Trustram Eve for his support and help with proofreading.

Disclaimer

This book is for general information about writing an undergraduate dissertation and it is not intended to replace the advice of your supervisor. If you suspect that you are suffering from stress and anxiety during the dissertation process you should consult your GP for a proper diagnosis.

Chapter One

What is a Dissertation?

A definition

A dissertation is an extended piece of work. It is an original work describing the process and results from a piece of research undertaken by the student. It is a chance to embark on your own research and can be the most rewarding part of a degree. However, it is also probably the first time that you've had to tackle a substantial and original piece of work, which can also make it the most stressful part.

An undergraduate dissertation is usually around 10,000 words long and it is organised into chapters. Like an academic book, it should have sections such as a 'Contents Page' and 'Bibliography'. You will have a set amount of time to produce your dissertation, which will give you enough time to research your topic and write up the results; chapter 3 examines managing your time in more detail.

One of the most important points about a dissertation is that it should be about a topic that interests you. The more that you enjoy the process of researching your dissertation the more you will take from the experience. Choose your subject carefully and don't rush into it; chapter 2 covers how to choose your subject in more detail.

'The more that you enjoy the process of researching your dissertation the more you will take from the experience.'

Dissertation or thesis?

The terms 'dissertation' and 'thesis' are sometimes used interchangeably. The name used will also vary depending on which country you are in. In the UK, it is generally accepted the term 'dissertation' is used for undergraduate study, where as a 'thesis' is associated with postgraduate study, especially a PhD. There will be some variability in this, especially with master's degrees where the dissertation is sometimes called a thesis.

What a dissertation isn't

▥ The dissertation isn't an excuse to avoid work until the last week. If you have left everything until a week before it is due, it will be practically impossible to complete it. However, if you are struggling with completing your dissertation, see chapter 10.

▥ The dissertation isn't a place to put forward all of your personal opinions. It is your own research, but it is still within a context. Be critical in your writing, but be professional and objective. Back up your theories with examples and citations.

▥ The dissertation isn't a piece of work that you do as part of a group. It is *your* research.

Who writes a dissertation?

The Higher Education Statistics Agency states that in 2011/12 there were 2,496,645 students in higher education, of whom, 1,928,140 were undergraduates. The vast majority of these students will have to write, or will have written, a dissertation. The dissertation is a piece of research that a lot of people have done; that doesn't make it any easier for you to do, but it does mean that you are not alone in writing it.

Undergraduate degrees are assessed in different ways, but most degrees will have the dissertation as the main part of the assessment. There is no escaping it. If you are studying for a degree you will have to write a dissertation. If you go on to study for a master's or PhD you will have to write more dissertations/ theses – they will just be more in-depth and longer. If you can learn the basics now, you will have the building blocks to go on to further study.

Mature students

Mature students and part-time students are making up a significant proportion of the current undergraduate and postgraduate student cohorts. At the University of York, up to 13% of the yearly intake is from mature students, in some departments this percentage is even higher. The issues facing a mature student writing a dissertation will be the same as a student who has come straight from school; however there might be a few differences depending on past experiences and current circumstances.

Mature students:

░ May have other demands on their time from family or another job, especially if they are studying part-time.

░ May bring a lot more experience to the process and therefore they might find certain aspects less challenging e.g. report writing, command of written language.

░ May find it hard to readjust to the learning process, with the dissertation potentially being the hardest part of all.

International students

The challenges faced by international students are immense. They are not only faced with the prospect of writing a dissertation, but often doing so in a non-native language. The issue of writing in a second language is one that is addressed differently at each university, there are often writing and language courses or sessions that can be taken. However, there may also be different cultural approaches to writing to overcome. In my experience this will vary enormously, but I once had a student who was heavily plagiarising. This was partly a language issue, but it came out later that it was more respectful in her native country to write out someone else's words verbatim, rather than paraphrase an idea and cite the idea as we would understand as the correct way to do it. This book will not go into detail about how to approach a dissertation if you are a non-native English speaker; but it does outline what is expected from a dissertation from a basic perspective, which should be helpful.

Why write a dissertation?

There are a number of reasons why we have dissertations:

- The dissertation is an opportunity to bring everything together that you have learnt during your degree course; from how to analyse and assess data, how to read critically, how to argue for a case and how to write succinctly and persuasively. By the time you write your dissertation you should have had a chance to practise all these skills in previous work.

- The dissertation marks a transition from student thinking to academic thinking. It is one skill to be able to summarise someone else's arguments in an essay, but quite another to be able to present your research within its context. Arguably, the dissertation is the first step to the next level of study.

- It is the main assessment of your degree. This pressure doesn't help the writing process; but it shouldn't be something to worry about. As you work through this book, you should be able to understand what is expected of you and also how to achieve it. It is very easy to say – but try not to panic!

- The skills you use in writing a dissertation are transferable and will help you show your future employer that you are able to:

    1. Work to deadlines

    2. Write coherently

    3. Summarise other people's work

    4. Work independently

    5. Produce reports

    6. Undertake research

    7. Organise your thoughts

'The dissertation is an opportunity to bring everything together that you have learnt during your degree course.'

What is expected from a dissertation?

Every subject and every university will have different guidelines and expectations for a dissertation. Make sure you read your institutional guidelines and departmental guidelines before you even start thinking about your research subject.

Length

There will be a set word limit for your dissertation, usually in the region of 10,000 words. You will probably be allowed +/- 5-10% on the word count before you are penalised, but don't take this for granted. By structuring your dissertation and assigning a word limit to each section you should be able to avoid going over the word count; see chapter 4 for more information on structuring your dissertation. Be strict with yourself. In my experience there is nothing worse than reading a good piece of work and having to penalise it because there are too many words. Make sure you leave time for editing and you should be able to reduce your word count when you redraft or edit your dissertation (see chapters 7 and 9 for more help on writing style and the end processes, respectively).

Structure

On a general level, all dissertations will contain these sections, although they might be called something different, or some of the sections might be combined:

- Abstract
- Contents and lists of figures/tables
- Introduction
- Background or Literary Review
- Method or Methodology
- Results
- Interpretation
- Conclusions
- Appendices
- Bibliography

A more detailed examination of all of these chapters can be found in chapter 4 and chapter 9.

Language and style

Every subject will vary, but by the time you come to write your dissertation you should be familiar with the style and language expected by your subject. Use exactly what you have learnt from your essay and report writing and transfer it to your dissertation.

If you should be writing in the third person, e.g. 'It was found that the experiment was most accurate when the computer was switched on', rather than the first person 'I thought the experiment was most accurate when I switched on the computer', make sure that is what you do throughout. It might not seem like there is much difference between the two sentences, but there is. Some of the most common mistakes are examined further in chapter 7, along with a simple explanation of why they are wrong and how to avoid them.

'Use exactly what you have learnt from your essay and report writing and transfer it to your dissertation.'

Where is the best place to start?

The first few days or weeks of trying to work out what you would like to research can be hard. Where do you start? Some people will know exactly what they want to research and will get off to a flying start; if that isn't you, don't worry. Start by looking at chapter 2 which will talk you through how to choose your dissertation subject.

Once you've decided on your subject, you need to think about the end. This may sound strange, but take a look at chapter 9. It's important to realise from the start that you will need to have a bibliography in a standard format, that you will need to have your dissertation bound in a certain way and if it's going to be 50 pages and you need three copies you're going to need to set aside some money and time for printing! None of these aspects are vital right at the start, but they are very useful to have in mind as you go along. It would be awful to get to the end of the project, read the submission guidelines and realise that the copies you've printed need to have a 2.5cm margin, not the 1.5cm margin of your document.

Once a subject is decided – what next?

Often the very first sentence that you write is the hardest. It doesn't matter how many ideas you have or if you have planned it out in your head or on paper, the action of starting to write can be excruciatingly difficult.

The advice from Dr Kevin Walsh, Senior Lecturer at the University of York, is to just start writing. It doesn't have to be a masterpiece. In fact, if you know from the start that you will probably rewrite it later, it should make it even easier to write. Take the pressure off yourself completely. It's not what you write at this stage, but making sure that you just start writing.

It is also worth bearing in mind that you don't have to start at the beginning. Starting with the conclusion probably wouldn't be a good idea, but if you wanted to start with the methodology, then do it. Once the writing process has begun, everything else will become easier.

How do I support someone writing a dissertation?

There will be times when the dissertation process is hard, emotional and frustrating for the student. It can be tough watching someone you care about go through those emotions. The best way to support someone is to have an idea of what they are going through and reading this book should help to highlight some of the problem areas and ways to overcome them.

What are the biggest concerns of students?

Having an understanding of the main concerns is a good place to start. You do not have to provide answers, but there might be ways you can offer support.

A recent study by Akister, Williams and Maynard in 2009 found that students' main concerns, before starting their dissertations, were: time management, ability to structure the dissertation, library skills and writing skills.

Issues that concerned students before starting their dissertations

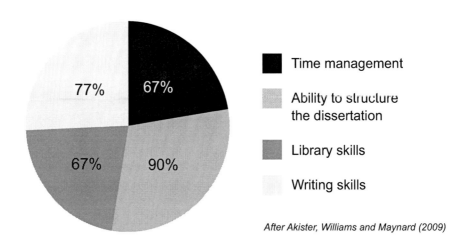

After Akister, Williams and Maynard (2009)

How can I help?

Think of yourself as a pair of braces holding up a pair of trousers. You need to offer support that is subtle but effective. There is nothing worse than a pair of brightly coloured braces worn over the top of a jumper, stealing the limelight! You want to be hidden away, quietly supporting and allowing the spotlight to fall on the fabulously fitting and stylish trousers, or more to the point, on the person you are supporting.

If you have an understanding of the issues, then you might be able to help with a solution. For instance, if the student's writing skills need some work, you might be able to help them with their grammar, do some proofreading for them or know of someone who can.

The pie chart shows some of the issues concerning a student when they *start* a dissertation, but the most stressful stage is likely to be towards the *end* of the writing process. Chapter 8 looks at ways the student can help themselves to get through the stressful periods. However, there might be ways that as a parent, partner or supervisor you can help too, such as ensuring the student:

- Takes regular breaks
- Takes regular exercise
- Eats healthily

Summing Up

- A dissertation is one of the first opportunities a student gets to embark on an original piece of work; it should be in a subject that interests them. Almost every degree student will write a dissertation. Most students will probably find that they have the same problems writing a dissertation.

- The dissertation often forms the main assessment for a degree; it is the chance to bring together all the skills you have learnt over the past three or four years.

- Every institution and subject area will have requirements; however the majority will contain specific sections, e.g. introduction, method, results, interpretation and a conclusion. It is usually 10,000 words long and is composed of set chapters. The writing style and language should be academic in nature and should be similar to previous work completed.

- Early on in the process make sure you understand the whole process of writing a dissertation, including what needs to happen at the end. This may save you a lot of time, heartache and possibly money in the long run.

- Start writing as soon as possible, even if it is gibberish. It's not *what* you write at this stage, but making sure that you *start* writing.

- It isn't always easy to know what support to give someone writing a dissertation. If you are in a supporting role think of yourself as a pair of braces holding up a pair of trousers. You need to offer support which is subtle but effective.

Chapter Two

Embarking on the Project

The very process of just starting the dissertation can be daunting. How do you know what you want to write about, or even where to start? Importantly, you should choose something that you have an interest in. You will be spending a lot of time researching and writing the dissertation, so make sure that the subject is something that you care about. There are other considerations too, but try to keep asking yourself, 'Am I really interested? Do I really care?' If the answer is no, then you should question whether you will have the motivation to write a dissertation on that subject to the best of your ability.

'Choosing a subject you enjoy will be a key factor to having a successful dissertation.'

What subject?

Take a piece of paper and a pen, and then start by asking yourself these questions:

- What subjects have I really enjoyed studying so far?

- Are there any particular topic/themes/areas within this subject which I have enjoyed? What are they?

- Are there any essays or seminars which I really seemed to have grasped or I've achieved a good mark for? What are they?

- Equally, which are the subjects that I haven't done very well at or that I haven't enjoyed?

This isn't going to provide you with an instant answer, but we'll return to the answers to these questions later. Don't be afraid to put down more than one answer to each question. The trick here is to be honest. Choosing a subject you enjoy will be a key factor to having a successful dissertation, but there are other factors that come into consideration too.

What type of dissertation?

A dissertation can take many different forms between and within disciplines. Knowing how you like to learn and what you enjoy doing, can also help in deciding what type of dissertation you want to write. Most dissertations fall into two categories, 'practical' (factual) or 'theoretical'. There will almost always be some crossover between the two, but a dissertation is likely to be based around one more than the other.

> 'Facts and theories are different things, not rungs in a hierarchy of increasing certainty. Facts are the world's data. Theories are structures of ideas that explain and interpret facts. Facts do not go away while scientists debate rival theories for explaining them'. Stephen Jay Gould, *Discover Magazine*, 1981.

Practical

Depending on your discipline, practical dissertations are likely to be based around:

- Fieldwork
- Lab work
- Questionnaires/surveys
- Archive work
- Manuscript analysis

In these types of study you are creating data and writing up your findings. You will need to draw on a range of skills for this type of dissertation, such as interviewing, transcribing, photographing, drawing, laboratory skills, microscope skills, statistical skills, understanding and manipulating databases. Theory will play a small part, but it should be a part of the interpretation.

If you want to do a practical dissertation, you will probably find that, in general, you are a practical person, someone who likes to *do* things.

Theoretical

Theoretical topics tend to be based upon:

▨ Ideas

▨ Reviews

▨ Comparisons

▨ Critiques

The subject matter will be more abstract and based on concepts and ideas. Every discipline will have a body of theories and ideas that have influenced its development, the way it is studied and how it is studied. You will likely have studied the history of your discipline by the time you write your dissertation and so you should be aware of some the influential bodies of thinking that were in play in the twentieth century, such as Marxism, feminism and structuralism.

To undertake a theoretical dissertation you will need to like spending a lot of time in the library with written sources. You need to be able to: understand the context within which the piece was written, grasp and explain abstract ideas, relate ideas to practice and critique a theory by examining what works and what doesn't.

Combining theory and practice

The more you are able to tackle both of the theory and practical elements, the better your chances of getting a higher grade will be. When you are dealing with data (a practical dissertation) you will need to be able to interpret the results, for this you will need to draw on theory. Equally, a theoretical dissertation will be made stronger by using data and case studies to support it.

'The more you are able to tackle both of the theory and practical elements, the better your chances of getting a higher grade will be.'

Does it matter where I'm living while I'm writing my dissertation?

Think about where you are likely to be living while you will be researching and writing the dissertation. If you choose a subject where you will need to do practical work or use resources abroad, or even in another county, question yourself seriously on the practicality of it. Do you have the transport to get there? Can you afford flights, rail or bus fares? Is there funding available to help you? If so, are you within the deadline to apply for it?

Can the dissertation help me to achieve my career goals?

If you have a clear idea of a future career, consider carefully whether the subject of your dissertation will help you towards your goal. If you are studying International Relations for example, think about whether your potential subject of 'defence and security' goes well with the charity career you want to pursue. You might find that it does, but ask yourself the question before getting too carried away with the subject. Equally, while it is important to write critically and analytically, it probably isn't sensible to write a dissertation directly criticising the organisation that you hope to work for.

'If you have a clear idea of a future career, consider carefully whether the subject of your dissertation will help you towards your goal.'

You might be reading this and thinking, 'I have no idea what I want to focus on for my dissertation, let alone a future career.' Keep reading. This section is still relevant to you too. A dissertation demonstrates a wide range of transferable skills:

▧ Working independently

▧ Ability to research a subject

▧ Writing and presentation skills

▧ IT skills

▧ Ability to think critically

▧ Data analysis

The list goes on. The point is that at some time in the future you might want to highlight some of these skills in a CV or an interview, so keep them in mind while you are deciding on your subject. Don't just exclude a subject because it has a statistical element that you might not like. If statistics are only a small element of a wider subject that you enjoy it might be worth considering it, you never know when you might need to call on that skill in the future.

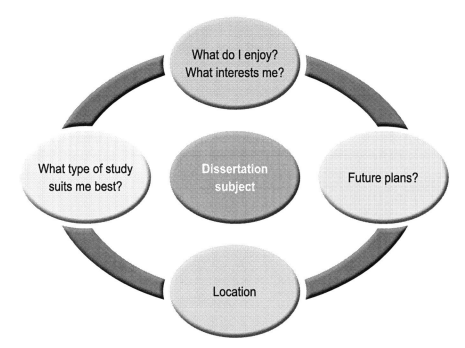

I have chosen my subject, now what do I do?

Often, choosing the subject is the easy part. The hardest element is deciding on the specifics: the title and the research question. This is made doubly hard by the fact that you have probably never had to choose a question or title for a dissertation before. If you've got to the point of having decided on a subject area, that is great news – you're halfway there. There are different ways on deciding your exact title; you might find that one or all these methods help.

Talk to a potential supervisor in that subject area

Don't be afraid to go to a member of staff and ask to talk to them about dissertation ideas. Once you know the subject area that you are interested in, make an appointment. Think about what you enjoy about studying that subject

'Often, choosing the subject is the easy part. The hardest element is deciding on the specifics: the title and the research question.'

and what interests you about it before you go to see them. Go armed with the answers from the previous section (about what you've enjoyed studying so far and why) they show that you have given it some thought.

Choose a title from a list

You might find that a potential supervisor, or the department/faculty, offer students dissertation titles from a list. This can be a double-edged sword in that a lot of the stress is taken out of the decision process, but you might end up researching and writing about a topic that doesn't interest you. If you are offered a list of titles to choose from, you should still go through the earlier section to think about what your interests are and the different types of dissertation that exist. Take your time before jumping in.

It might also be worth asking to change a title slightly if you think that taking a different angle would make it more interesting. You may or may not be allowed to do this, but it would be worth asking the question.

Read current literature on the subject

Once you have decided on a subject read everything you can get hold of about it. While you're scouring the library, also make sure that you are looking in relevant journals, magazines, newspapers and appropriate online forums. Although you need to keep focused on the academic writing, also look at the popular literature too – you never know where inspiration will spring from. Keep up to date with the subject in the broadest sense and also think about possible dissertation titles too, it might be that:

▓ The author of a journal article highlights areas for further research.

▓ Current events might make it timely to do a re-evaluation of a subject.

▓ A method used successfully in a study in one part of the country, might be relevant to an area close to you too.

Think about combining subjects/topics/interests

Again, go back to the first part of the chapter and look at what you identified as being enjoyable. Was there more than one subject? Think about links you can make between them. Also, consider what you enjoy doing outside of studying and what you want to do as a career. A friend of mine who studied Social Anthropology wrote his dissertation on the 'Anthropology of Street Theatre', due to his love of theatre and directing. He is now the Artistic Director of a theatre company.

Types of research

In Nicholas Walliman's book, *Your Undergraduate Dissertation: The Essential Guide for Success* (see the book list), he outlines seven types of dissertation question, which might prove helpful when you're whittling down your options:

1. Track through time – This is where you do 'a history of . . . ' and follow an idea, method, person, object, book, theme, etc. through time.

2. Describing – This type of work would involve looking at the features of something and classifying them. This type of work would perhaps be best suited to a science. Although you could also do a description of an organisation, person or an idea.

3. Comparing – Look for similarities and differences in a subject.

4. Correlating – This is looking for relationships between events, people or objects. You might also go on to look at possible causes of the relationships.

5. Evaluating – This type of study takes a set of criteria and compares a subject to them. You can start to measure qualities like efficiency and successfulness.

6. Intervening – This is where you take a known system and change it in some way to record the effects. This type of study is often used in developing new products or systems.

7. Simulating – make a simplified, often smaller, version of a real object or situation that you are studying. This is often carried out through models and experiments.

Support within your department

More and more university departments are providing guidance on the dissertation module with formal lectures, seminars, workshops and whole modules on the skills needed to complete a dissertation, including how to choose your title. If you are able to take advantage of these sessions, do so. Make them work for you by engaging with them as much as possible. The more work you can put in at this stage, the better.

How can I find out what is expected from my dissertation?

Look at previous work

Before I decided on my research question and dissertation title, I spent a long time looking through previous dissertations. Each year the person with the highest mark for their dissertation is awarded a prize and their name is put up on a board by the departmental office – where all the old dissertations are stored. I made a note of everyone who had won a prize over the last 5-10 years and read their dissertations.

Looking over previous work also comes in handy for chapter 4, chapter 6 and chapter 7.

What was I looking for? I had a list of questions:

- What was their subject?
- What was their title?
- How had they tackled their question?
- Was it easy to read? Why?

- Did it follow a logical structure? What was that structure?

- Had they answered the question they set out with, even if the answer was different?

Despite the list of questions, which was really useful, my main reason for looking through the past dissertations was to get a feel for them. I was trying to understand what a dissertation actually *is*, and how to tackle it.

The good ones were all easy to read, very well presented, thoroughly referenced with impressive bibliographies and kept closely to their subject. The subjects all varied enormously, but the level of detail and understanding shone through. I kept coming back to the previous dissertations whenever I was stuck. They would often help to give me an idea rather than provide the answer. While you're trying to find your dissertation title, they might do the same for you.

Grade descriptors

It is never too early to look at grade descriptors. If you've never seen them before, find out where they are located in your undergraduate handbook, intranet or ask for a copy in the departmental office.

If you're aiming for a high grade, you need to know what the examiners will be looking for. Make sure that the research question that you choose is broad enough to allow you to cover all of the main points needed to hit your target mark. If you need to be delivering original interpretation for a first class degree, make sure that your dissertation subject allows you to go beyond pure description into the realms of your own interpretation. Keep a copy of the grade descriptors close to you while you're writing, they will act as a reminder for what you need to be doing.

'It is never too early to look at grade descriptors.'

Summing Up

- Choosing the subject, title and research question of your dissertation can often be the hardest part. Whatever you choose it needs to interest you. Start by asking yourself which subjects you have enjoyed studying so far.

- Spend some time thinking about the balance you want between a practical and a theoretical dissertation. Do you like doing things or thinking things through? Do you like spending time in the lab or the library?

- Don't forget the practical considerations too. Where will you be living? What access will you need to the library or other material? What are your career plans, how does your dissertation fit into those?

- When it comes to refining the subject of your dissertation, start talking to potential supervisors sooner rather than later, read as widely as possible, and think about combining different subjects for an interesting angle.

- Early on, look at past dissertations and grade descriptors to get a feel for what is expected from your dissertation. They may also help you to focus on your question.

Chapter Three

Planning the Way Forward

Who?

The 'who' aspect at this stage falls into two main categories: your supervisor and other people associated with the research (interviewees, curators, lab technicians).

Supervisor

By this stage you may have chosen, or have been assigned, a supervisor and have had a preliminary meeting with them. Even if you haven't met with your supervisor yet, in these early stages you need to know how the student/ supervisor relationship will work.

Your relationship with your supervisor is important, work at it straight from the start.

- In any email correspondence, err on the side of formality rather than informality and avoid using text speak.

- Be presentable when you go to a meeting! First impressions are formed within seconds of meeting someone, be neat, clean and tidy.

- Have enthusiasm for your research; it's far easier to help someone who appears to be interested than someone who is disinterested.

- Go to the meeting prepared. Think about what you want to get from the meeting, prepare some questions or points to discuss.

Some departments will have a type of contract or dissertation agreement form that both you and your supervisor will sign at the first meeting. It may seem a little daunting, but the idea of it is to give you and your supervisor a clear

'Your relationship with your supervisor is important, work at it straight from the start.'

framework to work within. It helps to manage expectations from the start. Even if you are not expected to complete or sign an agreement, there are a few elements of it that are worth talking through with your supervisor at your first meeting:

- Agree a timetable – Your supervisor will likely have teaching commitments, administrative duties, planned sabbatical, marking, other dissertations/ theses to supervise, research to undertake and write up. This means that for you to get the most out of their supervision you need to know how your dissertation fits into their wider schedule. Make sure you stick to appointments and give your supervisor plenty of notice if you want them to look at draft chapters.

- Frequency and length of supervisions – Try to establish how much time you will have with them and split it down into chunks where you are likely to need it most.

- Agree the title – If you haven't already, you should agree the title and topic of your dissertation. Listen to and evaluate your supervisor's advice. This might be hard to do if you already have a clear idea of your topic in your head. However, your supervisor will also be thinking about your dissertation from a research perspective. They have experience of the research process, understand the resources and they are well acquainted with the mark scheme. If you don't take on board their advice, have a clear (academic) argument as to why you haven't. It's *your* dissertation; you need to be happy and clear about it.

'Listen to and evaluate your supervisor's advice.'

Remember that a supervisor is there to help you, but it's your work.

A supervisor CANNOT	A supervisor CAN:
Tell you what you need to do.	Help you when you ask for it.
Proofread your dissertation.	Provide guidance on content and structure.
Ensure that you pass.	Advise on where and how to make changes.

Other people related to the dissertation

If you need to arrange appointments or get access to material/equipment, then you should plan to do this early on. Be considerate to other people. They have lives too, they may be on holiday, working flexitime or be on paternity or maternity leave. The earlier you start talking to the key people involved in your study the better.

What?

Aims and objectives

The terms 'aims' and 'objectives' should be familiar to you by now, they often appear in written information about modules, lectures and seminars. They are also terms that are used frequently in businesses and other organisations, as well as within academia. Therefore, it is well worth getting to grips with these terms now as they will undoubtedly appear again at a later point in your career.

What is the difference?

Sometimes the terms 'aims' and 'objectives' are used interchangeably, or one without the other. They do, however, have specific meanings. In the broadest sense, the aim is what you are trying to achieve and the objectives are how you are going to get there.

An example

Title: 48 Hours to Change the World of a Six-Year-Old.

Aim: To successfully redecorate a child's bedroom in a weekend.

Objectives:

- To research an appropriate colour scheme, taking into account practicalities, cost and the appropriateness for a six-year-old.

- To source and use appropriate techniques/materials to remove the old wallpaper and repaint the room.

- To surprise the child with a new room after they have been staying with grandparents for the weekend.

In Appendix 1 (page 115) you will find an example of the aims and objectives from Robin Wilson's first class undergraduate dissertation.

Five points to consider when you are writing your aims and objectives

'At the end of your dissertation you need to be able to assess whether you achieved your aim, therefore your aims need to be measurable in some way.'

1. Don't start writing your aims and objectives until you have read through the rest of this chapter. Even then, you might still want to go away and look at the literature again or arrange a meeting with your supervisor.

2. Keep your aim general. Think about, 'What am I trying to achieve?'

3. Three is a good number of objectives to have, but the actual number will vary depending on discipline, supervisor and the subject of your dissertation. It is OK to have more, but the point is to try to distil your dissertation down. What are the main things that you will be doing?

4. At the end of your dissertation you need to be able to assess whether you achieved your aim, therefore your aims need to be measurable in some way. When you are writing your objectives, think carefully about the verbs that you use, e.g. to collect, to establish, to evaluate, to identify, to produce and to revise. Also think about what the real outcomes of these will be at the end; will you:

- Collect data?

- Establish a link?

- Evaluate two ideas?

- Identify a pattern in the responses?

- Produce a new method?

- Revise the interpretation of a site?

5. Writing your aims and objectives is hard. To write them you need to have a thorough understanding of your dissertation, which early on you are unlikely to have. *This isn't a reason to not write them!* Write out your aims and objectives now, but keep revisiting them.

Why?

You need a rationale, or a statement about why your dissertation topic is suitable, relevant and why it should be examined. You need to cover aspects such as:

- Why the question is important/interesting.

- Why the question hasn't been examined before.

- Why it is timely that this subject is researched now.

The best way to work out the answer to this is to:

- Ask yourself, why you are interested in the problem.

- Go to the literature review (see chapter 4) and think about how your work will fit alongside the work that has already been done. Will it fill a gap? Add more detail to an area? Bring a subject up to date?

How?

When you're thinking through how to undertake your research, you're actually thinking about your method. In chapter 1 we looked at different types of dissertation, practical or theoretical, and also different types of research. With your chosen type of dissertation in mind, you now need to think through the practicalities of it and you should include a short methods statement in your research design or dissertation proposal.

What do I include in the methods statement?

This is where you write about what you will be doing. You should include:

▨ How you will access any background literature that is difficult to get hold of.

▨ What data collection methods you intend to use.

▨ What methods you will use to analyse your results.

▨ Any potential problems that you can predict.

What problems are you likely to encounter?

You are not trying to come up with a perfect method. Not everything will work. If something goes wrong – it's OK. If you can predict the tricky areas, do that now. Even better, if you can predict what might go wrong, explain why you might encounter the problem or how you will overcome those problems – it shows that you have thought through the whole process. Also, when you come up against the problems, you won't be so surprised so hopefully they will be less stressful.

For example: You might be doing an assessment on water quality and need to take samples from two different rivers. However, the day before you are due to take your samples there is an issue with contamination from a nearby factory. Now, depending on your title, the contamination might provide an interesting discussion point or you might need to have another river in mind.

How to avoid problems:

Following are some examples of likely problems for certain dissertations.

▨ Fieldwork – Always allow extra days.

▨ Interviewing people – Always allow extra time and have other people in reserve.

▨ Literature reviews – Make sure you have alternative sources you can use if the original ones prove unsuitable or are unavailable.

- Laboratory work – If the experiments prove unsuitable or go wrong, is there another one you can use instead?

- Samples – Always take more than you need.

- Dealing with people – Always be able to explain your work and what you are doing. If you are going to be working away from the university you might encounter the public. Keep some identification with you and also, if you think it will help, a letter from your supervisor explaining what you are doing.

Try out your proposed method

If it is appropriate and you have the time, you could undertake a small pilot study to demonstrate your methods of data collection and analysis. This will help you to work out if the method is appropriate, whether it will work and where the potential problems might lie. You might have already carried out similar work for earlier essays or projects, if you have, refer to that work. Make sure you reference any previous work, even if it's your own.

Keep coming back to your objectives

Your methods should relate directly to your objectives. If your objective is to collect data, be explicit and say so:

Objective 2: To collect data on the resident bat population at Elm Tree Farm.

Methods statement: 'I will collect data on the bat population at Elm tree farm (Objective 2) by using three non-invasive survey methods: presence/absence survey, activity surveys and automated activity surveys at height, as defined in the Bat Conservations Trust's publication *Bat Surveys: Good Practice Guidelines* edited by Lisa Hundt (2012).'

When?

Creating a calendar/timetable/schedule will make you appreciate how quickly time disappears between now and the submission date. Start from submission and work backwards, making sure you leave a good chunk of time at the end for pulling it all together, proofreading, binding, etc. (see chapter 9). Not all

'Creating a calendar/ timetable/ schedule will make you appreciate how quickly time disappears between now and the submission date.'

disciplines or departments require you to include a timetable as part of the proposal/research design, but it is a vital stage of the planning process. Even if you are not required to do it, I would highly recommend spending some time thinking it through.

Be honest with yourself when you're writing out a timetable. Are you on holiday for a fortnight in August? Do you have a part-time job that means that some evenings or weekends have to be left free? Do you have other courses or exams running alongside writing the dissertation? Include every commitment you can think of in the timetable and make sure you leave time for switching off and relaxing.

Practicalities

When you're planning your time, also think through the practicalities of your dissertation. If you need to do fieldwork at a particular time, or if the people you are interviewing are only available at certain times, remember to work this into the timetable at the appropriate point.

Be realistic

Don't overestimate how much you can achieve. I always like to think that I'm highly efficient and I can fit everything into an allotted time period. However, unless I consciously build in 'run over' time, nine times out of ten I find I will have underestimated how long a task will take me. Also, other commitments and unexpected incidents do crop up; plan time for these. If it turns out you don't need that extra time you can get ahead or take a well-earned break. If however, you lose a day's worth of data because someone accidently turns off the computer in the lab, you know there is the contingency time.

How to present the timetable

Everyone works in different ways; in reality some people like lists and calendars, and others hate them. Either way, if you need to present a timetable as part of a research design or dissertation proposal, then you need to find a way to make it interesting to you. My partner hates the to-do lists that I create at every opportunity. If he needs to remember to do something he may put a reminder on his phone's calendar or find an app that can do it for him. That's his way of making timetabling relevant and interesting to him.

When it comes to presenting a timetable for the research design, a list of dates and tasks might suit you. Alternatively, you might be artistic and prefer to sketch a flow diagram with dates attached. Or, you might be highly organised and enjoy using planning software and so presenting your timetable as a Gant chart might be more suitable. However you do it, the timetable needs to be well thought through and realistic, don't be tempted to just make something up.

Give yourself a weekly goal

By breaking a larger task down into smaller pieces it makes it more manageable and you are less likely to become overwhelmed by it all. If you can give yourself weekly tasks as you go along, this will help you to feel like you are achieving something. Realistically, it will be hard to plan weekly tasks from the very start, but you should be able to give yourself tasks for the first few weeks based on your timetable. Include these tasks in the research design as they show you have an understanding of what's involved and that you are managing your time effectively.

Make the tasks specific. For instance:

- Write 500 words of the literature review before dinner.
- Finish the first phase of interviews this week.
- Make sure all the figures are finished and labelled correctly by Friday.

Summing Up

- Once you have decided on your subject and title, you should write a research design to help you plan how you're going to tackle the dissertation.

- You should identify who the relevant people are in your work and contact them in a professional manner early in the research process.

- The aims and objectives will be the glue of your dissertation. Your dissertation is about meeting those aims and objectives. Your 'aim' is what you are trying to achieve and the 'objectives' describe how you are going to do it.

- What is the rationale for your research? From the background reading that you have started, you need to state why you are doing your chosen topic. Are you filling a gap in the subject? Testing a method on a new set of data? Bringing a subject up to date?

- Describe how you are going to undertake your research, what problems you might encounter and solutions to those problems.

- Devise a timetable working backwards from the due date. For the coming weeks, give yourself specific targets and include these in the timetable too.

Chapter Four

The Structure of the Dissertation

Getting the structure to your dissertation right is like making sure you follow a recipe for baking a cake. You can have all of the right ingredients, but if you start to bake the flour and eggs before you put in the sugar and butter, your end result will be anything but a cake. However, if everything happens in the right order then at the end you will have a product, whether it is a cake or a dissertation, which is instantly recognisable.

A good structure allows your ideas and arguments to be easily followed by any reader. It will also help you to formulate your ideas and to plan your time. Think about your structure early on in the dissertation process and how your work will fit into it. In turn, this will help you to get your ideas across clearly and logically.

This chapter covers the main types of dissertation and takes a closer look at the type of information that needs to go in to each section. From this chapter you should be able to start putting together your own structure and gain the confidence to start writing.

'A good structure allows your ideas and arguments to be easily followed by any reader.'

Different structures?

There are two main structures that you could use depending on your discipline. Consult your department's guidance notes and/or your supervisor if you are unsure about the type of structure to use. The first structure is more suited to a practical dissertation.

Structure one

- Abstract
- Introduction
- Literature review/background
- Method
- Results and analysis
- Interpretation/Discussion
- Conclusions
- Appendices
- Bibliography/sources

Structure two

The second structure is more focused on developing an argument, with the body of the dissertation being given over to focus on a particular argument or text. This structure is most appropriate for a social science-based dissertation, where it is more theoretical or text-based:

- Introduction
- Subject/text/theme/topic/ 1
- Subject/text/theme/topic/ 2
- Subject/text/theme/topic/ 3
- Conclusion
- Appendices
- Bibliography/sources

Regardless of the structure you choose, every chapter should make sense if it is read in isolation, but it should also contribute to the overall aim of the dissertation. Think of each chapter as being the petal on a flower, with the flower being the dissertation.

Each chapter needs to have an introduction outlining what is going to be written about and how it will help to fulfil the objectives. Don't expect every chapter to fulfil every objective. You then need to have the body of the chapter, which contains the detail and a conclusion that demonstrates how that chapter has advanced your argument. Specifically, state how the chapter relates to your objectives and your overall aim (see chapter 3 for a reminder on aims and objectives).

How do I keep a theme running through the dissertation?

Much of the next section is about breaking the dissertation down into manageable chunks. It is useful to think of the dissertation as a series of smaller parts, like chapters of a book, scenes from a play or tracks on an album. It makes it more manageable.

Occasionally though, try to distance yourself from the work and read through some of the earlier chapters to check that there is an overall theme running through it. The theme should be your aims and objectives. It can be hard to distance yourself from your work but as Mike Sowden, Storytelling Consultant, says, 'Think of it as a single piece of work, and try to arrange it in a way that always provides a compelling reason for the reader to keep turning the page. That sounds like a no-brainer, but academic work is usually put together from blocks of discrete work and it's easy for it not to flow and have a "plot arc".'

Are there any common elements to a dissertation?

There are some elements of a dissertation that will remain the same, regardless of your discipline or dissertation subject. All dissertations need an introduction where you set out your aims and objectives, a meaty middle where you put forward your data, ideas, theories or findings and a conclusion where you summarise what you've done and what you've found.

As the quote by Dale Carnegie goes, 'Tell the audience what you're going to say, say it; then tell them what you've said'. This doesn't mean you need to know (and state) the conclusion in the introduction; the research process isn't that straight forward. You will read, write, rewrite, re-read and rewrite again before you arrive at a conclusion.

In the context of a dissertation, it would be better to replace the word 'say' with the word research: 'Tell the audience what you're going to research (introduction), research it (main body) and then tell them what you have researched (conclusions)'.

What tense do I use to write my dissertation?

Writing style is covered in more detail in chapter 7, however, it is worth thinking about the tense of each chapter in the early stages. I remember getting very confused as to whether I was writing in the past or present tense. Most academic writing is written in the present tense, e.g. 'Smith (2007) *presents* evidence of . . . '

However, there are exceptions to this in the dissertation. The tense that each section should be written in is outlined below.

Introduction

The introduction is about setting the scene. Initially, write your introduction based on your dissertation research design or proposal (see chapter 3). It might cover:

- The aims and objectives.

- Why you are doing the research: bringing a subject up to date, filling a gap, using a new method on older material, etc.

- How you will do the research, the types of methods will you use.

- Any hypotheses you have.

However, when you have finished the dissertation, revisit your introduction. It is likely (and probably best) that you will want to rewrite it so that it acts as a good precursor for what you've *actually* written, rather than what you *thought* you were going to write. No matter how well you have planned your dissertation it is highly probable that one or more aspects of the research will have changed while you are doing it.

Tenses to be used:

Present – E.g. 'The aim of this dissertation *is* to . . .'

Future – E.g. 'It *will* be argued that . . .'

A body of research and interpretation

This is where you 'research it' and tell us about it. The central chapters, regardless of how they are structured, form the bulk of your dissertation, whether they are based around chapters such as the literature review, methods, results, analysis and interpretation, or around case studies, arguments or texts. This is where you provide evidence of your thinking, argument and interpretation. The following sections outline some of the main points you should try to cover in each section, along with the style of each chapter.

Literature review/background

The literature review isn't a summary of everything you've read. It needs to be a targeted piece of writing that situates your dissertation in its context. You might decide to have different sections that review the literature in relation to themes or according to your objectives.

According to Birmingham University's Steve Gould, a good literature review ' . . . is critical of what has been written, identifies areas of controversy, raises questions and identifies areas which need further research' (http://library.bcu.ac.uk/learner/writingguides/1.04.htm).

The exact structure that the literature review takes will vary between dissertations. However, three approaches that might be appropriate are:

1. Moving from the general to the specific. Start by reviewing the overall

'No matter how well you have planned your dissertation it is highly probable that one or more aspects of the research will have changed while you are doing it.'

subject of the dissertation, e.g. current themes and arguments and then examine how your research will fit within the current literature and finish by assessing the works that you are directly relating to your research.

2. Use your dissertation structure to form the basic outline of your literature review:

▨ Wider context of your study (= Literature review).

▨ How have other people approached the subject? Are you going to be using a particular method? If so, what is it? Why have you chosen it? Ensure you write about it in relation to other people's work, show examples of it working (= Method).

▨ What have other people found? Are there any inherent problems? (= Results).

▨ Is there a particular body of theory that will underpin your interpretation? Are there other works/sites/surveys/experiments that are very similar to yours? If so, critique them. This section needs to be about the work that directly relates to your study, it therefore needs to be the most substantial section (= Interpretation).

▨ Summarise the previous work and how it relates to/informs your objectives (= Conclusion).

3. Historiography. Look at work chronologically, finishing with your work and how it will contribute to the subject. Be careful that this type of review doesn't become too descriptive. Critically analyse each period of thinking, think about the subject, what was good/worked? What was bad/didn't work? Draw out the main elements of each period/type of thinking that you are using and focus on these more heavily.

Tense to be used:

Present tense – E.g. 'Recent studies (e.g. Trout 2006 and Cannon 2012) *show* that people are more likely to be happy if . . . '

Methodology

For your dissertation proposal or research design, you will have written a methods statement (see chapter 3). Don't be tempted to use this as your methodology chapter! Your methodology needs to be a description of what you did, so that someone else can come along and repeat the same process.

Elements to include:

- The materials you have used.

- A detailed description of the processes you used to gather your data and analyse your data.

- Any problems you encountered and how you dealt with them.

- Ethical considerations and how you dealt with them (see chapter 5 for more information on the ethical implications of your research.

Tense to be used:

Past – E.g. 'The statistical analysis *followed* Brown et al. (1997) . . . ', 'The questionnaire *was* composed of three sections . . . '

Results

Your results chapter needs to describe what you found. You need to keep it factual, to the point and objective. Depending on your subject, summaries are often best used. These could take the form of:

- Tables – showing total, percentages, averages

- Graphs – pie charts, bar charts

- Maps – plots of key points

- Quotes – key quotes from interviews

- Photographs/illustrations – photos of sites, processes, materials

- Text – summaries of responses

Ideally, you want a mixture of these forms. You want to get the key points of your results over in the quickest and clearest fashion. Make it easy for your examiner to understand your results. You don't want them to spend time hunting around and trying to work out what you found; they will lose interest and move on. For instance, if you have a bar chart showing the response rate to a questionnaire based on postcode, you will also need a couple of lines of text outlining the key points, such as the areas with the best and worst response rates. At this point you don't need to offer any explanation for the different response rates; you are just describing your results and using descriptive statistics to do so.

If you have a lot of raw data, for instance transcripts of interviews, you should put these into an appendix, not the results section. You can include selected quotes in the results, but these should be there to illustrate a point.

'Evaluate your results in terms of the objectives. Did your method work? If not, why not?'

Tenses to be used:

Past tense – E.g. 'Of the initial population, only six *were* left . . . '

Present tense – Use the present tense when you are referring to figures and tables, e.g. 'Figure 6 *shows* the decline in foxes in cities since 2006'.

Discussion

This is the most interesting part of the dissertation, both to write and to read. It is here that you can really start to have an opinion about your research. A note of caution, don't get too carried away! Keep coming back to your objectives and use them to frame your discussion. Evaluate your results in terms of the objectives. Did your method work? If not, why not? Using the sources from the literature review, contextualise your results. Do the results help to move the previous interpretations forward?

Tense to be used:

Present tense – Use the present tense in relation to your findings, e.g. 'an issue that *arises* from the results . . . '

Past tense – Use the past tense when referring back to your aims and objectives, or to previous work, for example, 'Previous work (e.g. Collins 2003, George 1999 and Clives 2008) *has shown* that . . . but the evidence from this study suggests this is not always the case'.

Subject/text-based middle chapters

If you have opted for structure two, a more social science-based approach, you will need to approach the middle section in a different way. It is worth reading the 'Literature Review' and 'Discussion' sections again, as these elements are likely to feature strongly in the middle chapters. Following are two different ways to approach the middle chapters.

Text by text

One option for structuring the middle section of the dissertation is to give a chapter to each individual text, manuscript or site that you are analysing. The advantage of this method is that you can thoroughly cover all the texts. The disadvantages, and in my opinion these outweigh the advantage, are that you are in danger of having a very descriptive dissertation when you actually want to be showing your analytical skills. Secondly, there is a danger of a lot of repetition using this structure. You would need to analyse each subject/text by theme and you would need to introduce and contextualise that theme each time. So if the theme occurs across three of the books, then it could be become very repetitive and clunky.

By theme

The alternative approach is to take a thematic approach. Identify three or four main themes in your subjects/texts, which together allow you to answer your aim and objectives and assign each theme a chapter. Each chapter then needs to be broken down further into an introduction of the theme and then a discussion of how each book/manuscript in turn relates to that theme. The conclusion of each chapter looks at the theme as a whole in relation to your aim and objectives. This approach allows you to be far more analytical. It does mean that there will be aspects of the book/manuscript that you will have to miss out, but as long as you stick closely to your aim and objectives, it shouldn't matter. You could always flag up the areas that you have had to exclude in your conclusion for 'further work'.

Conclusion

The conclusion is where you look back at your research and relate it to your overall aim and title. Summarise the key findings here, but any discussion of them should have occurred in the interpretation/discussion chapter. Think about:

- Did you fulfil the aim? If not, why not? Perhaps you found more than you initially expected, tell us about it.

- Have you identified avenues of future research? Often the process of undertaking research raises more questions than answers. Frame these positively as areas for further investigation and be specific about what they are.

'The conclusion is where you look back at your research and relate it to your overall aim and title.'

Tenses to be used:

Present tense – Generally use the present tense, e.g. 'The analysis of the questionnaires *shows* that . . . ', 'The implications of this finding *are* . . . ' There might be exceptions to this, for instance if you discuss future work (future tense), or refer back to previously published work or your aims and objectives (past tense).

Bibliography

There is a detailed discussion of the bibliography in chapter 7. It is worth noting here that every dissertation needs a bibliography or a reference list. Without one, the dissertation is unlikely to pass.

Front and end pages

There is a detailed discussion of the front and end pages in chapter 9.

How long should each chapter be?

The length of each section will vary depending on many different factors. To get an idea of how long each chapter should be:

* Look at some previous dissertations in your subject.

* For proportions, rather than actual word counts, look at a well-regarded journal article in your discipline that tackles a similar subject.

'Every dissertation needs a bibliography or a reference list. Without one, the dissertation is unlikely to pass.'

Summing Up

- There are two main structures that you can use, depending on whether you are writing a science or a social science-based dissertation.

- All dissertations will contain an introduction and conclusion, and a middle section covering a literature review, methods, results, analysis, interpretation and discussion. How the middle section is organised depends on your discipline and the structure you choose to use.

- Although it is useful to split the dissertation into chapters, use your aims and objectives to provide a linking thread throughout the dissertation.

- You need to write each chapter in a different tense: past, present or future. Generally, most academic work is written in the present tense, but some chapters require a specific tense, for example the methodology will be written in the past tense, as this is a description of what you did.

Chapter Five

The Research Process

Every dissertation is different and will require a particular type of research. However, there are some generic areas that every student will need to consider to some extent. Are you struggling to find literature? Is there just too much information? How do you organise everything so it all makes sense? How will you know when to stop researching and start writing? This section will guide you through the research process giving you hints and tips on how to approach your research to get the most from it.

I can't find some of the key literature

One of the biggest problems that undergraduates seem to face is not being able to find key texts. There are never enough copies in the library. In my view, not using the key texts and therefore finding your own literature is 1) more rewarding and 2) means that your reader will probably find the piece more interesting and fresher to read because you're not just regurgitating the core texts. You do need to know the main works on your subject, but there are other ways to get hold of them – be creative!

Get to know the library and librarians

The best place to start is the library. Most will now have Wi-Fi so you can look at online sources, but you will almost certainly have to consult texts that are only available in good old-fashioned books at some point and it's easier if you're in the same building as them. If the book is out on loan, there are a few options:

'One of the biggest problems that undergraduates seem to face is not being able to find key texts.'

- Get to know the librarians, find out when they usually restock the shelves, that way you'll save time searching the books to be re-shelved and/or the actual shelves if it's likely to be in the other place.

- Request it. If you're starting the literary review early enough then there should be time to look at it before you submit.

- Drop your supervisor an email. Don't moan that you can't find the book in the library – they will have heard that many, many times before. Be keen; say that you want to get on with your background reading, but that some of the texts are unavailable. Ask if they might have a copy or if they know of someone who does, and whether it might be possible to borrow it for a few hours. Some people are reluctant to loan out personal copies, but if you are only borrowing it for a few hours you are unlikely to take it away and never return it, so you might convince them to lend it to you. Also, a few hours will give you enough time to read selectively (see page 53), raid the bibliography (see below) and find out if you need to request a copy from the library. If you do borrow a personal copy, make sure you return it in the state it was lent to you and in good time.

- E-books. More and more books are now available as e-books through your university's online library pages or through services like Google Books.

- Second-hand copies. It might be possible to find a cheap second-hand copy online or in a student second-hand bookshop. You can always resell it when you're finished with it.

Raid bibliographies

The most useful research advice I was given as an undergraduate was to take the core reading, read it, go through the bibliography and then find some of the literature from the bibliography, read that and repeat the process. There are a few advantages to this:

- If there are three or four students with similar dissertation topics, this method will lead you to the original work and different case studies. This will make your work stand out from the others.

- It is demonstrating to your supervisor and/or examiner that you can think independently, use the library and research a topic thoroughly.

- It is potentially a lot more interesting to read the original articles, rather than another person's opinion of them (although summary papers are useful too).

Reading selectively

You will have a lot of background reading to get through. If you haven't already learnt to read selectively, you will need to start now. Harvard University has a very good document online called *Notes on skimming a book or reading selectively* (isites.harvard.edu/fs/docs/icb...files/tips_on_skimming.doc), which outlines the differences between reading for pleasure and reading for information and gives more tips on how to do it.

When you're reading with your literature review in mind you should be thinking about your title, aims and objectives. Think through what you want to know before you even pick up a book or read an article. Then you need to target your reading, don't just start at the beginning and read to the end. If you do, I can almost guarantee that you won't remember what happened at the start, because the amount of information/arguments/theories in an academic book is vast, the language is complicated and might be unfamiliar and the ideas will be complex. Instead, you need to target your reading as the diagram below shows and keep asking yourself, is it relevant to my work?

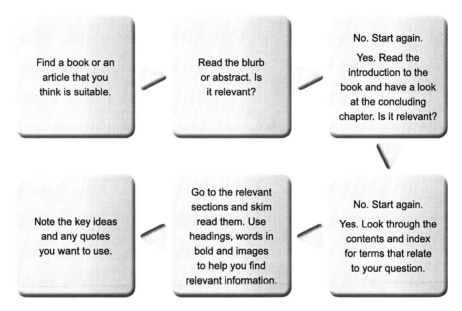

Find a book or an article that you think is suitable.

Read the blurb or abstract. Is it relevant?

No. Start again.

Yes. Read the introduction to the book and have a look at the concluding chapter. Is it relevant?

No. Start again.

Yes. Look through the contents and index for terms that relate to your question.

Go to the relevant sections and skim read them. Use headings, words in bold and images to help you find relevant information.

Note the key ideas and any quotes you want to use.

'Keep notes as you go along, they are invaluable.'

Keeping notes . . .

Keep notes as you go along, they are invaluable. The dissertation is a longer, more complex essay; if you have a good note-taking system for essays, use the same one for the dissertation. If you have managed to get through your degree so far without taking notes, now is the time to learn.

. . . on literature

Everyone has different methods by which they like to record information, you might choose to use a notebook or a laptop. It doesn't matter if you prefer electronic forms to pen and paper; you need a system for note-taking. First, when you take notes from a publication you are *not* trying to copy everything down, you might want to write out a quote in full, but generally you want to summarise the argument, list the examples they use and make sure you have all the bibliographic information (title, date, author, publisher, place of publication, journal title, volume and issue numbers, and page number). If you're finding it hard to take notes, ask yourself these questions:

▦ Can I summarise the last paragraph/section/page in one sentence?

▦ What themes does this case study illustrate?

▦ What is significant about this publication? Is it the first in-depth study? Does it illustrate a change in direction for your subject?

Ways you might find it useful to take notes:

▦ Buy a 5-section notebook and put each section over to a different subject/theme. When you come across a relevant text, make the notes in the appropriate section, using a fresh page for each new article or book.

▦ Use software like Microsoft OneNote, to organise your notes thematically.

▦ Use bibliographic software like Mendeley or EndNote. The advantage of this system is that you can save e-journal articles straight to the program, use it to compile a bibliography, annotate the articles and save notes to the reference.

. . . on methods

Your methodology might be entirely based upon accepted methods, in which case you may not need to take extensive notes. However, keeping a factual diary of what you did, will make writing the methodology section a lot easier. It doesn't have to be long or in-depth, but keep a note of events as they happen, especially if you are using a new method. The type of information you might record includes:

▦ Date and time.

▦ Any conditions that might affect your results. E.g. if you are asking people about their opinions on the current government and a tax increase was announced the day before, it will be useful to have a record of it.

▦ What you did, what standard methods you followed, what deviations you decided to take.

※ Anything that was significant that day.

. . . on data collection

For more scientific dissertations your notes on data collection are likely to be included in a lab or field notebook. This might be the place where you also record notes on the methods, as mentioned previously. Having your data clearly set out in one place and in a useable format can help you save a lot of time later on.

Come up with a form or table, before you start the data gathering and know that for every piece of data you need to collect the same information. It might be that you need to include metadata too, such as:

※ The name of the archive

※ The name of the collection

※ Any codes or ID numbers

※ The date you accessed the source

※ A contact for the archives

※ The condition of the material

This will help you if you need to go back to the archives because you forgot to make a note of something, or when you need this information for the list of primary sources you have used.

. . . on ideas

Ideas can occur to you in the strangest of places. I often find that my best ideas come to me when my mind is in neutral, usually as I'm falling asleep, in the shower or when I'm driving. All of those times are inconvenient for whipping out a pen and notepad and although I should keep a pad with me at all times, I don't. So how do I remember the ideas? I use my phone, which I almost always have with me.

※ I use a dictaphone app on my phone to record an idea as soon as I can safely pull over off the road.

- I make use of cloud computing and make notes in an app that synchronises with the Web or my laptop, so that when I sit down to write the notes are ready and waiting.

- I use the camera on my phone as a way of being able to remember information (rather than ideas) such as on a poster or if I need to remember a particular location.

I also use techniques to help my brain remember information, such as using numbers and letters as references. Or I try to hold on to one word that encapsulates the thought until I can get somewhere to record it. For example, if I am writing about the effect of fallow deer on residential gardens I will try to remember how many ideas I had and then focus on just remembering that number. Or, I will remember the first letter of each effect and then just remember those. Try it.

Are there any ethical implications of my research?

If your research involves people, you might need to think carefully about the following ethical issues:

- How will I store people's data?

- Am I creating data on a vulnerable section of society, e.g. children, elderly people or anyone with a mental or physical disability?

- How do I ask for and obtain consent? How do I record this?

- Do I need to obtain permission from an organisation before I interview its employees? What procedures do they have in place for this?

- How will I ensure that the data I obtain from people will be anonymous and confidential, or is the person happy to be named?

It is likely that as part of defining your dissertation you will address these issues with your supervisor either informally, or through an 'Ethics Agreement'. An Ethics Agreement is there to help protect you and the people you are researching. It is a document where you identify ethical issues and outline how you will address them.

> Every time you refer to someone else's ideas, arguments, general work or data, you must reference where you came across it.

Referencing and bibliographies

Every dissertation needs a bibliography or a list of references. A bibliography is a list of texts that you have referred to in your dissertation and can also mean all texts that you have looked at, not just referenced. Every time you refer to someone else's ideas, arguments, general work or data, you must reference where you came across it. Don't think that you can pass the work off as your own as this is deemed to be plagiarism and is taken seriously by all universities. Having marked a lot of students' work it is immediately obvious when a student has plagiarised something. From your first term at university you will have been given guidelines on how to reference properly and how to create a bibliography, spend time getting to grips with the system.

'Every time you refer to someone else's ideas, arguments, general work or data, you must reference where you came across it.'

Advice from Nick Trustram Eve, a former mature student:

'Sort out referencing ASAP and start using EndNote, Mendeley or whatever else is available. You can gradually build your own database of references and not have to worry about the formatting of references for the bibliographies. It takes away this headache completely.'

There is more advice on referencing and bibliographies in chapter 7

Knowing when to stop

It can be very easy to lose track of time (and your timetable) during the research process. There isn't necessarily a defined end point. This is especially so if your research has turned up something unexpected, or something that you find really interesting.

Set limits before you start

Always keep your research objectives close to hand. Also, regularly re-read them and check that what you are doing is really meeting the objective. By using your objectives as a pre-defined research framework, you can constantly check that your research falls within the boundary. This can be especially useful if you are the type of person that likes chasing leads and finding out new things. These new facts might be very interesting, but they are also probably tangents and you need to keep these under control as much as possible.

What do I do if I find there's more than I thought there would be?

You might be thinking, 'That's all very well saying that tangents need to be kept under control, but now I've started, I realise there is far more data than I expected.' For instance, in surveying people you might find that six of your questions are enough to fulfil your objectives, but now you have all of the data from the other twenty questions. What to do?

First, seek an appointment with your supervisor, they are there to help. They will probably suggest one of two things. If you are well ahead of schedule and the data is particularly interesting or controversial then they may suggest you include some of it. However, in the majority of cases, it will be far more appropriate to present only the findings from the relevant questions in a clear and concise format that answers the objectives you started with. You might then summarise the other data in a paragraph of your results section, or use it in your conclusion for the basis of further work. A key point to remember is that a dissertation is just the start of a wider research process, although you are expected to answer your objectives, you are not expected to suddenly provide a world-class, totally comprehensive study of your chosen subject. If you need a reminder of what you are trying to achieve, go back to your grade descriptors.

'A dissertation is just the start of a wider research process . . . you are not expected to suddenly provide a world-class, totally comprehensive study of your chosen subject.'

Summing Up

- All research is unique to you, but there are some techniques that can help all students when they are researching their dissertations.

- Finding the key texts for your subject can be tricky if there is one copy in the library and someone else has it. Be creative, use summary papers, online e-books, or ask around in your department if anyone else has a copy.

- Start raiding the bibliography to get back to the original studies/papers and to find new examples. This will help you improve your mark as you are going beyond the normal key sources.

- Keep notes on the literature you read, your methods, your data collection and ideas.

- Understand if there are likely to be any ethical considerations in your research, and address these before you start.

- Keep referring back to your aims and objectives to make sure the research process doesn't consume you. Really question if you need to do something if it doesn't help you address one of your objectives.

Chapter Six

Presenting and Analysing Your Results

When it's time to write your results and analysis sections you will need to draw on a number of techniques. When you present your results you need to *summarise* them. It is highly unlikely that you will present all of your raw data in your results section; instead the data will go into an appendix.

When you come to analyse your results you are putting them into context and saying what you think they mean. You can do this by:

- Putting your results into context and referring back to the work you highlighted in your literature review.

- Using statistics to draw inferences about how your data is indicative of wider patterns.

This chapter will take you through presenting and analysing your results, suggesting useful ways of describing and interpreting your results.

'When you present your results you need to *summarise* them.'

I have so much data, now what do I do?

Like I have said before, don't panic. Take your time and tackle it slowly. The likelihood is that you have spent a long time with your data: thinking about it, planning how to collect it and then actually collecting it. You are very close to it in an analytical sense, and now you need to step back from it.

First, look back at your objectives. What were they? Write them down. Now think about how your data fits those objectives. Think carefully if you actually need all of the data you've collected. If it doesn't help you to fulfil your objectives, it is worth questioning its place in your dissertation. Talk to your supervisor if you are questioning its merit.

Next you need to put your data into groups and summarise the findings.

Why do I need to summarise my findings, aren't they obvious?

You will be so familiar with your data that you will probably be able to spot the patterns almost instantly. Surely other people will be able to see these patterns too? They might be able to spot the patterns as well, but you need to demonstrate that you have recognised the patterns and that you are able to show their significance to your objectives. You need to summarise the information in a way that is objective and allows your examiner to think, 'Yes, they have a good grasp of the results and what they mean.'

'You need to summarise the information in a way that is objective.'

The best way to demonstrate the patterns in your data is to quite literally show them in their simplest form. For example, leave your examiner in no doubt that '75% of the participants (15 out of 20) in the survey aged 18-21 had undertaken summer work at some point in their lives, compared to only 60% (12 out of 20) of participants aged 30-40 years old, see Figure 1'.

Figure 1

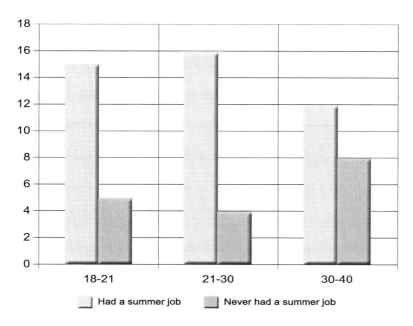

By writing the description and also including a summary chart or table, you are showing that you have recognised key features of your data and you are making it really easy for your examiner to see the pattern. You don't want to make them search out the pattern. This section examines how to present your results, both in the written form and using figures and tables.

Language

The language you use for presenting your results needs to be objective and descriptive. The 'Reporting Results' section in John Morley's *Academic Phrasebank* on the University of Manchester's website (http://www.phrasebank.manchester.ac.uk/) gives a good overview of the types of phrases and words you could use.

What are figures and tables?

Figures are all the drawings, photos and graphs in your dissertation. They occur more widely than just in your results and analysis, but a large percentage of them will be in these sections. Tables are the spreadsheet data that you insert from programs like Microsoft Excel.

Using graphs and tables to summarise your results is a good way to get your point across effectively. As the old saying goes, 'A picture paints a thousand words'.

If they are relevant, you might also want to include:

▪ Photos of your results

▪ Maps

▪ Plots of results

Including figures and tables breaks up the text and makes the chapter easier and more enjoyable to read.

However, when you're planning your figures and illustrations Dr Steve Ashby, University of York, warns against using pointless illustrations and ones that don't show what they claim to. Choose your figures carefully. Ask, 'Why am I using this? Do I need to?' If the answer is yes and the figure supports the point you have just made, then use it. If it's there just to look good, then leave it out.

When do I analyse my results?

If you are writing a science-based dissertation, your interpretation/analysis of your findings will come in the discussion/interpretation chapter, if you have one, not your results chapter. However, if you are writing a case study/text-based dissertation, the results and interpretation of that case study/text is likely to occur in the same chapter.

How do I analyse my results?

Draw up a simple table with the following questions and methodically work your way through answering the ones that are relevant to your research. You can then use the information from the chart to form the basis of your analysis:

- Have you summarised your main results?

- Have you interpreted your results? This isn't the same as describing them.

- What is the significance of your results? What do your results mean?

- Do your results answer your aims and objectives? How?

- Have you discussed your results in the light of previous research?

- What are the wider implications of your research?

- Were there any problems or limitations with your research?

- Were there any improvements you could make?

- Can you suggest any directions for future research?

When you are writing the analysis of your results, keep asking yourself, 'How did I come to that conclusion?' or 'Why do the results mean what they do?'

Dr Steve Ashby, University of York, says 'Don't just say something is interesting, you need to show *how* it is interesting.' The easiest way to do this is by using the linking word 'because'. For example: 'The results from the first experiment are interesting because they show . . . '

> 'You now have your results and you need to say how they reflect, challenge, support and add to the body of literature that already exists.'

Refer back to your literary review/background chapter when interpreting your results

The literary review sets the whole context for the dissertation: why the subject is important, why your study is important, the background to the method, the theoretical background, etc. Your analysis of your results should be like a mirror of your literary review, but with a slight distortion. You now have your results and you need to say how they reflect, challenge, support and add to the body of literature that already exists.

In chapter 4 there was an outline of what should go in a literary review. Refer back to this now and in conjunction with your own literary review ask yourself the following questions:

- How do my results fit into the wider context of your subject?
- Has my work illustrated a new method? Was it effective?
- Did I find the same as other researchers? Why or why not?
- What problems did I encounter?
- How do the theoretical arguments help you to interpret your results?

Aims and objectives

'Statistics are used as a way of making sense of data, of analysing data and presenting it.'

Return to your aim and objectives. You need to show your reader/examiner that you are addressing the questions you set out to answer. Be explicit when you refer back to your objectives, for example:

'The results from the interviews have illustrated that the weather affects the mood of 18-30 year-olds. These findings directly address Objective 1 of this research, which was to assess the impact of weather on the mood of undergraduates and recent graduates'.

You do not always need to restate your objectives, but it's useful to do so occasionally because:

- It helps you to bring your work back to the original objectives.
- You stated your objectives quite a few pages ago, there is no harm in reminding your reader what they are.
- You are demonstrating that you are answering the question. Doing this is vital if you want to get a good mark.

Statistical analysis

Statistics are used as a way of making sense of data, of analysing data and presenting it. This section will briefly explain the types of statistics that you might want to use in presenting and analysing your results. However, if you are using statistics I would recommend taking a module about using statistics for your subject area or finding a book that examines statistics for the sciences or social sciences. If you are in any doubt about whether you need to use statistical methods or not, then you should talk to your supervisor.

Samples and populations

Before you think about using any statistical analyses, you should understand that your data is a 'sample' of a wider 'population'. These are two terms that form the basis of statistics, so it's worth thinking about what they mean.

The people that you interview, or the trees that you measure for your research, are only a proportion of all of the people or trees in the world or in the forest. They are a 'sample'. From the 'sample' you are trying to understand the 'population'.

A 'population' is the wider group that your 'sample' is a part of. e.g. all of the trees in the world or all of the trees in the forest. To be able to put forward your suggestions about the wider populations, based on the results of your sample, you need to use inferential statistics.

Usable Stats has a good tutorial online at: http://www.usablestats.com/tutorials/basicStats, which introduces you to the basics of statistics from the start.

Descriptive statistics

At the simplest level you have descriptive statistics. These are statistics that you can use to help you describe your data and are ideal for the results section of your dissertation. These include:

▓ Mean – this is the average number

▓ Median – this is middle number

▓ Mode – this is the number that occurs the most often in the data set

For example, if you had measured the heights of a group of nine hazel trees and you found that they measured:

186cm, 200cm, 236cm, 236cm, 240cm, 260cm, 293cm, 305cm, 311cm.

The 'mean' is 251.89cm. You add up all the numbers and divide the total by the number of trees. The 'median' is 240cm; this is literally the middle number when all the heights are in order. The 'mode' is 236cm, because this is the most frequently occurring height.

Descriptive statistics are a way of describing your data, which is the sample.

Inferential/analytical statistics

If you want to go beyond describing your data (the sample) and use statistics to start making inferences or predictions about the wider population, then you'll need to use inferential statistics. This section just mentions some of the tests you might do; it does not tell you how to do them, as that would be a book in itself!

First you need to know whether your sample is likely to be representative of the population you are drawing inferences about. To do this, you would carry out a test of significance, which might be a chi-squared, ANOVA, Pearson's r or a t-test.

Don't worry too much about the names of the tests – this section is just to make you aware that there are a variety of tests you can run depending on the type of data you have and what you want to test for.

Most universities have software for running the various statistical tests, such as SPSS, R or Minitab. It is likely that your department or faculty will run a module or training session on statistics and using the software; alternatively your computing services department may run a training session. If you are at all likely to need to use statistics to analyse your results, book yourself onto the session or module.

Summing up

- Your results section/chapter needs to describe your results. Your analysis section/chapter needs to interpret your results and tell us what they mean.

- Tables and figures are a good way of summarising your results in a clear fashion. Just make sure that all tables and figures support your text.

- Use your literary review/background chapter as a reference point for your analysis/interpretation. How do your results fit with/support/contradict other work?

- Statistics can be a useful tool for describing your results (descriptive statistics) and for analysing your results (inferential statistics). If you think you might want to use statistics but are unsure about them, talk to your supervisor and also attend any training course/modules on using statistics.

Chapter Seven

Writing Skills

To achieve the best mark you can, you need to keep your reader focused on your results and ideas. To do that, the reader mustn't get:

- Lost in your argument – they need a logical thread to follow.
- Boggled by jargon – you need to make it easy to read.
- Distracted by grammatical errors and spelling mistakes.
- Confused about whether this is your idea or one that you've read somewhere else.

This chapter examines writing style and ways that you can get your point across in the most effective way.

Signposting your work

Signposting is all about letting your reader know what's coming next, so they're not surprised. I've just used the first sentence to tell you what signposting is, the title of the section is 'Signposting your work' so this introduction is letting *you* know that we will be looking at some techniques that you can use to help your reader 'guess' what's coming next.

Structure

In chapter 4 we looked at Dale Carnegie's quote, 'Tell the audience what you're going to say, say it; then tell them what you've said' in relation to structuring your dissertation. The same mantra also applies, on a smaller scale, to paragraph structure.

- You need to prepare your audience for the argument you will put forward.

'Signposting is all about letting your reader know what's coming next, so they're not surprised.'

- Present the argument.
- Tell your reader the gist of the argument or its implications.

Structuring your work in a set formula allows your reader/examiner to clearly follow your line of argument without even thinking about it. This leaves them time to absorb your arguments/ideas/research methods, which is where you'll pick up marks.

Use headings

By using headings within your chapter your reader knows when you are changing between subjects. Use headings and subheadings to help separate different ideas, just remember to bring them all together at the end of the chapter under a heading such as 'Summary' or 'Conclusion'.

Are there words that can be used for signposting?

One of the problems with undergraduate dissertations found by Dr Steve Ashby, lecturer at the University of York, is 'the lack of linking words and signposts'. So what does a signpost look like? No, this isn't a joke. Signposts are words that show the reader what's happening next, telling them that we are moving forward, or referring back to something. Below are a few of examples of signposts:

- **This** – Refers back to the previous sentence
- **However** – Shows that you are now going to put an alternative idea across
- **In summary** – Informs your reader that you are about to summarise your points

Peter Redman and Wendy Maples have compiled a more thorough list at: http://www.sagepub.com/redman.

All of these examples might seem self-evident. It may seem obvious to stop at a 'STOP' sign when you're driving, but if you're mind has wandered, then the sign quickly gets you back on track. Signposting words act in the same manner for your reader.

What style should I write in?

Simple, yet scholarly

Most subjects have a collection of terms and phrases that are specific to it. Don't use one of these words unless you fully understand its meaning. For example, if you write, 'White (2007) uses a Marxist interpretation in his analysis of cat footprints', make sure you know what a Marxist interpretation is.

Don't try to make your writing sound more scholarly than it is. Your writing needs to be clear and easy to follow. Your dissertation needs to sit somewhere between scholarly writing and everyday colloquial language. Err towards more scholarly writing, especially as you become more familiar with the scholarly terms in your dissertation, but always keep it simple.

Scholarly writing	**Your Dissertation**	Everyday colloquial language

Although your supervisor isn't there to help you with grammatical issues, if they have read a draft chapter by all means ask them in your feedback session if you have hit the right tone/style.

Don't use contractions

This is a case of 'Do as I say, not as I do'. This book isn't a scholarly piece, it is meant to be written in a way that's accessible to everyone, so I've used conversational language. I've also used far more contractions than I would if I were writing an academic paper. When you write your dissertation, remember that you are not having a chat with someone. You are trying to show your reader that you are meticulous, thorough and professional. The language you use and the style the piece is written in helps you to do this.

'Your dissertation needs to sit somewhere between scholarly writing and everyday colloquial language.'

Use the third person

Read your university or department style guidelines if you're unsure whether you need to use the first person ('I') or third person ('it'). If in any doubt, stick to the third person in your writing. Some examples of using the third person are:

* *This* study will examine the differences . . .
* *It* was found that . . .
* The objectives of *this* dissertation are . . .

By using the third person, you are making your writing more objective and less personal. It also allows you to present a more balanced view.

Can I express my opinion?

'The language you use should *suggest* your ideas, not assert them as facts.'

Express your opinion in the discussion, provided that it is always supported by evidence and that you explain your reasoning. However, be careful how you state your opinion. After all, it is just that, an opinion. The language you use should *suggest* your ideas, not assert them as facts. It is almost impossible to prove without a shadow of a doubt that a fact or theory is 100% true, so don't try. Instead, express your ideas in terms of suggestions, possibilities and likelihoods.

For example:

* It *would appear* that the correlation between the data sets is caused by . . .
* A *possible* explanation for the anomaly is . . .
* The research presented in this dissertation *suggests* that . . .

Formatting

You need to format your work correctly before you print it and hand it in, but it is a lot easier to format the work when you first start writing. There is more information about formatting your work in chapter 9, so spend some time reading that chapter to find out more about:

* Page numbering

- Using headings
- Creating a contents page

If you use the 'Styles' available in the 'Home' tab of Microsoft Word for defining your headings you can see your work summarised in the navigation tab, which makes navigating your document a lot easier.

Grammar

Were you taught grammar at school? Do you remember any of it? A paper written by Hudson and Walmsley in 2005, *The English Patient: English grammar and teaching in the twentieth century* stated that: 'For several decades up to about 2000, most state schools in England taught little or no grammar, and it is still normal for school leavers to know virtually nothing about grammar'.

The lack of formal education in grammatical rules isn't an excuse for not learning! However, it does explain why many students suffer from poorly written dissertations. If you want to stand out above the rest of your peers, get to grips with grammar and use it correctly.

There is a very good grammar learning quiz on the LearnHigher website http://learnhigher.ac.uk/Students/Academic-Writing.html, click on 'Grammar Beagle'. The quiz takes you through a series of questions and at the end it not only tells you if you're right or wrong, but it shows where you went wrong and how to write the sentence correctly. By seeing a real-life example in action, it helps you to improve your own writing.

From marking students' work, the most common grammatical mistakes are:

- Capitalising nouns – Nouns (names of objects), do not need capital letters. I would often come across the sentences such as: ' . . . studying World history is relevant to...' The word 'World' does not need to be capitalised. The exceptions to this are formal titles of something, e.g. Great Britain (place), Margaret Thatcher (person), *Writing a Dissertation: The Essential Guide* (book title).
- Apostrophes in the wrong place – Apostrophes are used to show that something belongs to someone, for example: Smith's theory or Japan's

population. They are also used where a letter is omitted in a contraction, but you should avoid using contractions in your dissertation! Examples of contractions include: there's = there is, wasn't = was not, you'd = you had.

- Confusing it's and its – 'Its' is the exception to the previous rule about possession. If you are showing possession, then 'its' doesn't have an apostrophe, e.g. the laboratory has its own equipment. 'It's' with the apostrophe, is used in the same way as the contractions above; it shows that a letter has been missed out, e.g. it's = it is.

Another common mistake, according to Dr Steve Ashby, University of York, is sentence structure. More specifically, he finds that students commonly use run-on sentences or fragment sentences.

Fragment sentences

A fragment sentence is only part of a sentence. Every sentence needs three parts: a verb (a doing word), a subject (who or what is having something done to them) and the sentence needs to make sense, which is usually done by including an object (something that is being acted upon). If you are missing one of these elements the sentence will not make sense and it leaves you asking, 'What?'

To illustrate a fragment sentence Dr Steve Ashby uses, 'For example, York Minster'. You are left thinking, 'What about York Minster?' You need more words in the sentence. Try to read each sentence in your dissertation in isolation and ask yourself if it makes sense. If it doesn't, it will need more words.

Run-on sentences

A run-on sentence is usually two separate sentences put together as one without any punctuation.

A run-on sentence:

'The results of the test show that osmosis was occurring osmosis is the process by which water and other molecules move through a membrane'.

This should be two sentences with a full stop after 'occurring':

'The results of the test show that osmosis was occurring. Osmosis is the process by which water and other molecules move through a membrane'.

If there is merely a pause in the flow of an idea, or a change in direction indicated by words like 'but', then a comma or a semi-colon might be used instead:

The results of the test show that osmosis was occurring, but at the same point the day before the process had yet to start'.

Spelling

It almost goes without saying; make sure you use a spellchecker for all of your work. However, it's worth also using the 'Find' function to look for all of the words in the section 'Common spelling mistakes' and check you have the correct version.

Common spelling mistakes

A spellcheck will only return words that are misspelt. It won't find words that you have accidently misused. When someone (especially an examiner) is reading your dissertation, you don't want any negative thoughts to pop into their minds, even if it is only 'I wish they had proofread this.' Get it right early on and keep checking for spelling and grammar niggles.

Common typing errors include:

- There/their/they're
- From/form
- Thorough/through/though/thought
- Has/had
- Complied/compiled
- Choose/chose
- Summaries/summarise
- Weather/whether

'It almost goes without saying; make sure you use a spellchecker for all of your work.'

- Of/off
- You/your/you're

Why are citations important?

This section is potentially the most important part of the book. Using citations can make the difference between your dissertation passing and failing. You could have a brilliantly written dissertation, but if you don't use citations then it will be almost impossible to pass. Use your essays and draft chapters to perfect your use of citations.

What is a citation and how do I use it?

'Using citations can make the difference between your dissertation passing and failing.'

When you mention someone's ideas, facts or anything else that you have gleaned from a book, article or website, you need to say where they've come from. The vehicle you use for doing this is a citation. The exact style or format of the citation will vary depending on the referencing system that your university uses. The example below is based on the Harvard system, but check what system you should use.

The citation generally includes:

- Surname of author/s
- Year of publication
- Page number/s

To give a real example:

'In the 1600s the claret-producing districts were beginning to gain individual identities as traders started to assign high values to certain areas and producers', (Kay and Maclean 1985, 67).

The information above is paraphrased (reworded) from page 67 of the book by Kay and Maclean. Notice that the citation comes at the end of the sentence, but before the full stop. Also notice that there is no comma between the names of the authors and the year of publication. These may seem like small details, but they are part of the system and your reader/examiner will be very familiar with the system, so pay attention to detail and get it right.

There are different ways of formatting a citation depending on:

* If there is more than one author.

* If the publication doesn't have a named author.

* If there is no date for the publication.

* If you are referring to ideas that spread across more than one page.

Seek out your university's guidance on referencing, print it out and always have it to hand. If you use someone else's research in your work and you don't put a citation after it, this is called plagiarism. Plagiarism is taken seriously by all universities, because it is effectively stealing someone's ideas and passing them off as your own. Always use citations!

What is a bibliography or reference list?

Sometimes the terms 'bibliography' and 'reference list' are used interchangeably and sometimes they have specific meanings. A bibliography is a list of all the books that you have cited in your dissertation, plus any other sources you have consulted. A reference list is purely a list of the sources you have cited in your dissertation. Check with your dissertation guidelines or your supervisor which one you need to supply.

Regardless of which you need to create, you have to record every book used for citations. Depending on the referencing system you use you may need to supply the information in a different order or style. The general information that you record includes:

* Author's surname and initials

* Date of publication

* Publication title/article title

* Name of the journal – for articles

* Volume and issue of the journal – for articles

* Page numbers of the article – for articles

* Publishers and place of publications – for books only

'If you use someone else's research in your work and you don't put a citation after it, this is called plagiarism. Plagiarism is taken seriously by all universities.'

If you have cited a chapter in an edited volume, a website, newspaper, magazine or report then the citation information will be different again. Learn the style, what information you need, what needs to be in italics and where the commas/full stops occur.

Is there an easy way to keep track of the sources I use and take the hassle out of remembering how to format a citation?

There is a lot to remember to get citations and reference lists in the correct format. The more you do it the easier it becomes and if you do it as you go along it just becomes part of the writing process.

Another step to making sure you get the formatting correct is to use software to manage your citations, such as EndNote, Reference Manager or Mendeley. Often, universities will have arrangements to provide one of these free or at a reduced price for students. Mendeley is free to anyone.

The software acts as a database for everything you have read. You can manually enter the publication information, or can import it. Most bibliographic programs link with Microsoft Word, so that once you have chosen your reference style, you just click on the publication you want to cite and a correctly formatted citation will appear in your Word document. You can also use these programs to generate a list of references.

Summing Up

⬚ Don't let poor spelling and grammar mask your ideas. Make the reading experience as easy as possible for your examiner.

⬚ Signpost your work, by using a standardised structure, headings and subheadings and signposting words to show what's happening next, when the text is moving forward or referring back to something.

⬚ Use simple, but scholarly language. Don't use contractions or colloquial words. Equally, avoid using academic jargon unless you know what it means and it's appropriate.

⬚ Use the third person (it) not the first person (I) throughout your work. This helps to make the work objective.

⬚ Try to avoid fragment sentences and run-on sentences.

⬚ Check your work for spelling mistakes and common typing errors.

⬚ Learn how to use citations properly and use them whenever you are referring to someone else's ideas or work.

⬚ Think about using bibliographic software such as EndNote, Reference Manager or Mendeley to keep track of your citations.

Chapter Eight

Looking After Yourself

Think of yourself as an old car. A car will get you from A to B, but you stand a much better chance of arriving at your destination if you've looked after your car, filled it up with oil (that was why I said an *old* car!), topped up the windscreen wipers and had it serviced. By looking after yourself mentally and physically you will find that the quality of your work improves because you will be sharper and more focused. This chapter outlines some simple ways to help stay in shape while you're writing your dissertation.

Breaks

It seems counterintuitive to take breaks, but make sure you do, especially towards the end when the writing process becomes more intense. Dr Hayley Saul, a recent PhD graduate said, 'I was told, when I was writing my dissertation never to think about it unless you are sitting next to your notes. Make sure you switch off; because your productivity becomes much lower if force yourself to carry on. It worked for me!'

Surely I'll get less done if I take a break?

By taking regular breaks during the day you are allowing your brain to switch off for a while, so that when you come back to your task you're fresher. John P. Trougakos, an assistant management professor at the University of Toronto, Scarborough, Canada said that, 'Mental concentration is similar to a muscle . . . It becomes fatigued after sustained use and needs a rest period before it can recover . . . much as a weightlifter needs rest before doing a second round of repetitions at the gym.' (Source: New York Times http://nyti. ms/LcUmnU).

'By looking after yourself mentally and physically you will find that the quality of your work improves because you will be sharper and more focused.'

If you find yourself starting to check your email or surf the Web, then stop. Take a proper break away from your computer allowing yourself a 15-minute break and then go back to the task.

I've booked a holiday, but now I feel I ought to be working . . .

As well as taking a few minutes off during the day, you also need to give yourself days off. If you've booked a holiday part way through the dissertation writing – take it! If you haven't, seriously consider taking some time off. An article by Julia Rampen on the website 'Workplace Savings and Benefits' reports that a quarter of British people feel more productive when they come back from a holiday. However, it might be best to avoid taking time off in the last week or two before your due date, unless of course you have everything finished!

Food

The food and drink that you put into your body not only affects your weight, but it also affects:

▪ Your mental capacities

▪ How alert you feel

▪ Immune system

NHS Choices has 8 key tips for eating healthily:

1. About a third of your diet needs to consist of starchy food, bread, potatoes, rice.

2. Eat lots of fruit and vegetable. It's worth remembering that these don't have to be fresh, they can be tinned or frozen, which is often cheaper, especially when you're living on a student budget.

3. Eat a couple of portions of fish a week. There will be more this on page 86.

4. Reduce the amount of sugary foods and those that contain saturated fat.

5. Reduce the amount of salt that you eat.

6. Drink more water. More on this later.

7. Take regular exercise. More information about this in the 'Exercise' section on page 89.

8. Always eat breakfast.

The following sections go into more detail about some of the points that are particularly relevant to you as a student.

Drink water

Drinking water can boost your energy levels, especially if you are dehydrated. Keeping hydrated keeps you alert and stops you feeling tired and sluggish. The best drinks for keeping you hydrated are water, milk and juice. Tea and coffee are fine to drink, but be aware that they only act as a temporary stimulant; your water intake shouldn't be made up of entirely tea and coffee.

Brain food

There are certain foods which are good for your brain, as well as being good for your general health. A recent article by BBC Good Food listed the following foods as being good for your brain; my comments follow each food type as a suggestion for finding cheaper ways to access these foods, or comparable alternatives:

- Blueberries. Some supermarkets now sell blueberries as a value brand.

- Broccoli. In spring you can often find purple sprouting broccoli more cheaply in a local greengrocers than in the supermarket. It's also likely to be fresher and more local too. Alternatively, it might be cheaper frozen.

- Tomatoes. If you are cooking with tomatoes, use tinned varieties. They taste better because they are often grown in warmer climates and they can be cheaper.

- Vitamin C. Personally I find that keeping my levels of vitamin C up, really helps me feel more alert. Vitamin C can be found in citrus fruit, blackcurrants, tomatoes, mangos and nettles. When I'm writing I cut out the

'Keeping hydrated keeps you alert and stops you feeling tired and sluggish.'

caffeine and drink nettle tea (nettles free from my garden) and blackcurrant. You might laugh, but try it (just make sure the nettles aren't from the side of the road and are not in an area where dogs walk!).

- Oily fish contains essential fatty acids, which are great for the brain. Oily fish types include salmon, trout, herrings, mackerel, sardines and kippers. Try trout, it is often cheaper than salmon but tastes similar. Or, if you're grabbing a sandwich for lunch why not try sushi instead? In the main cities sushi bars often produce delicious fresh sushi that's cheaper than a good-quality sandwich.

- Nuts and seeds. These are great for snacking at your desk, rather than binging on chocolate! Buy in bulk from health food stores for the best value packs.

What type of work station do I need?

'Having a comfortable place to work is vital both for your wellbeing and for your motivation.'

Having a comfortable place to work is vital both for your wellbeing and for your motivation. I really like to have a window nearby, as I start to get claustrophobic if I can't look outside! Equally, having your work table/desk and computer set up properly is vital for health and your comfort.

Your desk

It's important to create space to work in. It might be a desk at home that you can arrange as you want to, or it might be that you take your 'desk' with you and work at the library. Either way it's important to find a space that you like to work in, where you can concentrate and feel at ease.

Sitting position

If you sit in the same position at a computer for a long time, you may start to encounter aches in your back, neck and wrists. These pains might be prolonged or short-lived, but it's best to avoid them altogether. Not only might they affect your health in the longer term, they are a definite distraction in the short term.

Get your work area set up so that it's comfortable for you. One of the main problems is working with laptops. The top of your screen should be at eye height. With laptops it's often considerably lower so that you can access the keyboard. Consider getting an external keyboard that you can plug in and then use heavy books or a sturdy box to prop up your laptop to the correct height.

The other common problem is not having your forearms horizontal to the desk. If you are able to, find a surface to work at that allows your arms to rest naturally in the horizontal position, or use a chair with the ability to adjust the height.

Eye strain

If you are using a computer for long periods, it's important that you don't strain your eyes. There are a few things you can do to help your eyes:

▨ Take regular, short breaks. These are better than less frequent, longer breaks.

▨ Have your screen an arm's length away from you.

▨ Keep your screen free from dust and smears so that you can focus properly on the screen.

▨ Set the zoom so that the words on the screen are easy to read.

▨ Avoid glare on the screen by not having the monitor or yourself facing direct sunlight.

▨ Set the contrast and brightness of your screen so that they match the light conditions in the room.

'Take regular, short breaks. These are better than less frequent, longer breaks.'

Keep warm

If you're writing your dissertation over winter and early spring, it is easy to get cold if you are sitting still for a long time, especially if your workspace is in a cold or draughty area or you suffer from bad circulation. Keep warm and keep the circulation going by:

- Getting up from your desk frequently to move around.
- Drinking warm drinks.
- Wearing extra layers.
- Keeping a hot water bottle on your lap on in the small of your back.
- Wearing fingerless gloves when you're typing.
- Finding somewhere warm to work, like the library or a coffee shop.
- Doing some exercise; going for a short, brisk walk or doing some vacuuming will soon warm the extremities.

I feel like I'm always working, surely that can't be healthy?

As well as taking regular breaks, there are also other things you can do to look after your general health while you're working on your dissertation:

Sleep

When you're working to get something finished like a dissertation, there will inevitably be some late nights involved. It's important that you get enough rest; otherwise you will have only succeeded in making the following day a write-off. No matter how late it is, spending a few minutes winding down before you go to sleep can make the difference between getting a good night's sleep and tossing and turning because your brain is still buzzing with thoughts about what you've just been doing. Read a book, watch TV or listen to music, do whatever makes you relax and switch off.

Stress

There are often enough stresses while you are at university, without the added pressure of the dissertation, which is stressful in itself. Stress can be recognisable by being more irritable than normal and having sleep problems. There are ways of coping of with low-level stress, such as:

- Dealing with the problem that you're stressed about. If you're worried about seeing your supervisor, or you're stuck on how to interpret your results, deal with it sooner rather than later. You'll feel better once you have, even it's hard to do.

- Try to take breaks from your work and force yourself to relax by doing something entirely different, e.g. watch a film or read a book. Doing something different that occupies your mind, will force your brain to relax.

- Get regular exercise and eat healthily.

If the stress and anxiety continue, go and see your GP.

Exercise

Exercise can help you focus, which, when you're researching and writing about an in-depth subject is a good thing. When we exercise, our brain creates new cells, and these are vital for helping us to keep focused on a task.

Exercise can be in many forms, if you are already part of team or go to yoga classes, try to keep up with this commitment. It's not only giving you a break from your academic studies, but it's also helping them! Alternatively, if you don't really do much exercise at the moment, then try something quite gentle, like walking. If you're in doubt about the level of exercise you should take talk to your GP.

'When we exercise, our brain creates new cells, and these are vital for helping us to keep focused on a task.'

Summing Up

- It's important to look after yourself while you're researching and writing your dissertation. Not only will it help with your general health, but by looking after yourself mentally and physically you will find that the quality of your work improves because you will be sharper and more focused.

- Take short breaks regularly. There is no point forcing yourself to continue working if your mind is wandering. Take a short break and then return to the task.

- Take days off; again, these will help you to focus when you return to the dissertation.

- Eat a balanced diet, avoid too many caffeinated drinks and drink lots of water. Foods that are particularly good for your brain include: broccoli, oily fish, nuts and seeds, foods containing vitamin C (citrus fruits, nettles) and berries.

- Get your workstation set up so that it is a comfortable place to work, make sure you are sitting correctly and your monitor is clean and at the right distance from you.

- Keep yourself warm. Take regular breaks to warm up by going for a brisk walk, or use a hot water bottle to keep your core body warm.

- Always try to wind down before you go to sleep: meditate, read a book or watch some TV.

- If you feel like you are suffering from stress (you are irritable and having problems sleeping) then try to deal with the problem that's causing you the stress: make sure you take some 'down time' from your work and get plenty of exercise. Consult your doctor if the problems continue.

- Take regular exercise, it's good for your brain!

Chapter Nine

Finishing the Dissertation

Now you have finished all the main chapters, which are certainly the bulk of the work, but unfortunately you can't relax yet. It would be like someone offering you a toasted sandwich, but it arriving untoasted. Getting the final stages completed in the right way can mean the difference between a few marks or even the difference between passing and failing, when it comes to having a complete bibliography. Most departments or faculties will have a set of guidelines or a style sheet for how to set out your dissertation, which you should use.

What other sections do I need to include?

Your guidelines will list the sections you need to include in your dissertation. These sections are effectively the bread of a sandwich. You want your examiners to enjoy reading the whole thing, so make sure you have all the correct 'bread' around your main chapters.

Write the end sections before writing the front section as you will be adding page numbers when you create the end sections, which will affect the table of contents.

End sections

At the end you may wish to include:

* Appendices, so that you can present some of your raw data.
* Bibliography or reference list. The bibliography is an absolute must, without one you are unlikely to pass.

'Getting the final stages completed in the right way can mean the difference between a few marks or even the difference between passing and failing.'

Some universities will ask you to put the bibliography or reference list before the appendices – check your guidelines. You use the same page numbering system for the end sections as you do for the main body of the dissertation.

Front sections

The front sections, or preliminaries, may include:

- A title page – With the title of the dissertation, your dissertation number (not your name) and the date of submission.

- An abstract – A short summary of the whole of your work.

- Table of contents.

- List of figures – This is like a table of contents, but purely for the illustrations and diagrams your dissertation.

- List of tables – This is also like a table of contents, but for all the tables in your dissertation.

- Acknowledgements – Where you thank everyone who helped to support your work. Remember to include your supervisor and anyone who has given you access to archives/data/interviews, or helped in anyway.

'The bibliography is an absolute must, without one you are unlikely to pass.'

You should use a different numbering system for the preliminary front sections, ideally use lowercase Roman numerals, e.g. i, ii, iii. And switch to 1, 2, 3, 4, etc. in your introduction.

What does it mean when I'm told I need to format my dissertation?

Formatting is about the layout and arrangement of the page, it is about creating a standardised look to the page, so that all the titles are the same size, the page numbers exist and are always in the same place, and it generally looks consistent.

'A lot of students seem to be scared of using Word's headings and format their work inconsistently,' says Dr Steve Ashby, leader of the dissertation and research skills modules at the University of York (Archaeology Department).

If you format your document at the start (i.e. establish what size font you will use, what your line spacing is, etc.) it will save you a lot of time at the end. If you are not already familiar with formatting a long document, have a look at the video by SimonSezIT.com on YouTube: http://www.youtube.com/watch?v=WzTwfs_bbt8.

Page numbers

Word will automatically add page numbers for you, click on 'Insert', then 'Page Numbers'. There are a few things to watch out for:

▒ Page numbers (and fonts) can change if you work between different computers. Add the page numbers and contents page on the computer you will use to print.

▒ You need it to start page numbers from your Introduction. To do this click 'Insert', then 'Page Number' then 'Format Page Number', then click 'Start At' and choose the page number you want it to start at.

Use styles to create headings

In the 'Home' tab, you can use the 'Styles' to consistently format your headings. It is best to use 'Heading 1' for your main headings, e.g. Introduction, Methods, etc. and 'Heading 2' for subheadings. If you need to create more layers of information you can use 'Heading 3' and 'Heading 4'. There is detailed information in the help list at the end of the book on how to create headings using styles.

Number your chapters and sections

Numbering your chapters and sections can make your work easier to follow. Start numbering at your introduction, for example, '1. Introduction' and number the rest of your chapters sequentially.

When you start a new section within the chapter put a decimal point (a full stop) and then restart the numbering again e.g. '1.1 Aims', '1.2 Objectives'. This level of heading is the equivalent of using Heading 2 as a style; the two go hand in hand (see the previous section 'Use styles to create headings'). You can continue to use more decimal points as you go deeper into a subject, but try not to go beyond using three or four, as your argument is likely to get lost if you create too many levels.

You can also get the heading style to automatically apply a multilevel numbering system, which will enable you to create a table of contents at the end. A good explanation of how to do this can be found by going to YouTube.com, search for '1.2.1. Multilevel heading' and click on the video by 'WhiteRAZOR'.

Create a contents page

The other advantage of creating headings is that you can use these to generate a table of contents. Move the cursor to where you would like the table of contents to appear. Click on the 'References' tab in Word and then click on 'Table of Contents'. You have the option to choose from two automatic tables, select one of them. Your table of contents will appear. If you need to make any changes to your text, the table won't automatically update, you need to right click on the table and then click on 'Update Table', choose 'Update entire table', then click 'OK'. At this point any alterations you've made will appear.

Two points to remember when you create a table of contents:

- You can edit the table of contents like any other text, for instance you can change the font, alignment or spacing. However, some of the formatting disappears when you update the table, so it is best to finalise the formatting at the very end.

- The table of contents will automatically create the table from the preset styles: Heading 1, Heading 2 and Heading 3. If you need to include Heading 4 and beyond, you will need to insert that table differently. Click on 'References', then 'Table of Contents' and this time choose 'Insert Table of Contents . . . '. A window opens and click on 'Show Levels', here you can choose how many levels you would like it to show.

Numbering and labelling figures and tables

In the same way that you have numbered your text, you also need to number your figures (all drawings, photos, graphs and charts) and tables. Figures and tables need to have a separate numbering system and need to be labelled. The caption should always state:

- Whether it's a table or figure.

- The number of the figure or table. Usually the chapter number, followed by a decimal point and then start the numbering again, e.g. the first figure in chapter 1 would be, 'Figure 1.1'.

- A title.

- Any citations or copyright information that's relevant. If you have scanned and included a diagram from someone else's work you need to cite them in the same way that you would a piece of text, including the page number.

An example of a caption from '2. Methods' could be:

Figure 2.1 Illustrating the process of mineral extraction. (After Smith 2012, 12)

How do I number figures and tables?

Microsoft Word allows you to add figure and table captions. Go to 'References' and click on 'Insert caption'. From this window you can select the label to be applied from the options: an equation, a figure or a table. Also, if you click on 'Numbering' you can also select your chapter numbers to be used for the first digit of the caption number. The numbering function will only work if you have used the 'Styles' mentioned previously. It is worth playing with the captioning feature as you go along, as it can take a bit of getting used to. The key to it working properly is getting to grips with 'Styles'.

Create a 'List of Tables' and a 'List of Figures'

A list of tables and a list of figures is essentially a contents page but for the non-text parts of the dissertation, e.g. images, diagrams and tables.

'Figures and tables need to have a separate numbering system and need to be labelled.'

Using Word's 'Insert caption' tool (see page 95) gives you the option of automatically generating a list of figures and a list of tables. Click on the 'References' tab, then 'Insert Table of Figures'. In this window you can change the 'Caption Label' to 'Figure' or 'Table', which will create a list of figures or tables, depending on which one you choose.

The advantage of automatically creating and numbering your captions is that when you insert a new image (and therefore a new caption) it will update the numbering for you. If the numbering hasn't updated automatically, right click in the figure number and then click 'Update field'.

If you need to change the font, spacing or size of the caption, don't do this manually because when you update the table it will disappear. Instead, go to the 'Home' tab, then scroll through the list of styles until you see one called 'Captions' right click on it and select 'Modify'. From within this window you change the font, size, spacing, position, etc. to your liking.

Don't forget ...

Once you have finished writing there is a temptation to think you're done. There are a few little jobs still to do:

Spellcheck

'Use the spellcheck function; if there's a red squiggly line then check the spelling,' says Dr Emma Waterton, Senior Lecturer in Social Sciences at the University of Western Sydney. It may sound obvious, but you'd be surprised how many people submit work without spellchecking it.

Also, check that the default language for the spellchecker is English (UK), not English (US). You can do this by clicking on 'File', then 'Options' and then 'Proofing'. Then click on 'Custom Dictionaries' and choose 'English (UK)' from the drop-down menu of languages.

Proofreading

When you are proofreading you should be looking for lots of things, spelling mistakes, grammatical mistakes, missing words and questioning 'Does it make sense?' It is hard to proofread your own work, so ask someone else to read it through. You can also try out these techniques too:

- Find a quiet room and read your work aloud. Dr Emma Waterton suggests that this 'is the surest way of catching those pesky run-on sentences and incomplete sentences. If it doesn't make sense as you are reading it aloud, it is unlikely to make sense on the page.'

- Switch on the speak function in Word. I have a terrible problem of missing out words as I type and I can't spot the omissions. So what do I do? I listen to it being read back to me by an auto-reader. To access the text-to-speak function, add it to the quick access toolbar at the very top left-hand corner of the screen. Click on 'File', then 'Options', then 'Quick Access Toolbar'. Select 'All Commands' from the drop-down menu called 'Choose commands from' and then scroll down to 'Speak'. Click 'Add' and then 'OK'. A button showing a speech bubble and a play arrow appears in the toolbar. Just highlight the text you would like to have read back to you and press the button. You might want to use earphones if you're working in a public place.

Rewrite your introduction and write your abstract

Your dissertation needs to address what you set out to do in your introduction. By the time you've done your research, written chapters and then rewritten them, it's likely that you've actually ended up in a slightly different place to where you thought you would. This is absolutely fine and is part of the research process, but go back to your introduction and check that it introduces what you've actually done.

At the very end write your abstract, if you are required to write one. This needs to summarise your whole dissertation, including your conclusions and is usually no longer than 200 words.

'Go back to your introduction and check that it introduces what you've actually done.'

Check all your citations are in your bibliography/reference list

Read through your dissertation and check that the source of each citation is in the bibliography. Put a tick by each reference in the bibliography as you go, that way you can see which ones haven't been directly referenced.

Check your contents page

Last of all; remember to update your table of contents and your lists of figures and tables.

Printing and binding

'It is important to get the quality of printing and binding right.'

It is important to get the quality of printing and binding right and also to leave enough time for it happen. Think about the cost of printing and binding as well. Either buy supplies gradually to spread the cost or put some money aside each week. It is worth buying the best quality paper you can afford, especially if you have a lot of illustrations – you want to make them look the best they can. Experiment with types of paper until you get the look you want.

Printing

Don't underestimate how long printing can take with refilling paper trays, changing ink cartridges or toners and fixing paper jams. If you are printing at home buy more ink and paper than you need, but keep the receipt so you can return any unopened packets.

Binding

Establish who is going to bind your dissertation a few weeks before your deadline. It is highly probable that there will be a lot of other people also trying to get theirs bound at the same time. Call the binders to find out when they are open and what lead-in time they need, don't expect to be able to turn up and for them to be able to do it while you wait.

I've handed it in, now what do I do?

The first thing you need to do is celebrate! You should be immensely proud of what you've just done; a huge amount of work has gone into the dissertation. Some people feel elated that it's finished, others feel a sense of anticlimax and, 'Now what?' Everyone is different. Either way, you need to look forward to what's next; it might be exams or getting back to work or family life or figuring out what to do. But before you move on:

▨ Make sure you do take time to celebrate finishing the dissertation; it's part of the moving-on process.

▨ Drop your supervisor an email or pop by to say thank you. They will really appreciate it.

▨ Clear your desk and put everything away from the dissertation, it's time to do something different now.

Summing Up

- Although the main body of the text is finished there are still a lot of little bits to finish off. These are often quite time-consuming.

- As well as the main chapters of your dissertation you also need front sections (a title page, contents page, list of figures or tables and acknowledgments) and end sections (a bibliography/reference list and appendices at the end).

- The entire document should be formatted for consistency. The best way to do this is to use the 'Styles' in Word. From these you can also then create a 'Table of Contents'.

- The figures and tables need to have captions. The easiest way to create these is to use the 'Insert caption' function in Word. This also allows you to create an automatic 'List of Figures' and 'List of Tables'.

- Go back and update your introduction; and write the abstract.

- Before you finish, don't forget to spellcheck and proofread the whole document. Also check that all of the sources you have cited are in your bibliography and update your contents page.

- Leave plenty of time for printing and binding.

- Last of all, celebrate handing in the dissertation – you've finished!

Need2Know

Chapter Ten

What to do if Time is Running Out

You could find yourself in one of two circumstances.

1. You've done your research and some draft chapters but there are only a few days left before you need to hand in your dissertation. It feels like there is still half of it to write, there are parts of it that you would like to rewrite, proofreading to do, binding . . .

2. You haven't done any research or writing and the deadline is in two weeks.

This section is primarily about coping with the first situation; where you have the data, but there is now very little time left to finish writing it. The most important thing to remember is that you need to hand in a complete piece of work, rather than a dissertation that's missing the conclusion because you ran out of time.

'If you are starting from scratch and the deadline is looming, you need to go and see your supervisor immediately.'

You haven't started and there's only two weeks left

If you are starting from scratch and the deadline is looming, you need to go and see your supervisor immediately. I appreciate that this is far harder than it sounds. Prepare yourself before you go, know that it will be a hard meeting, but if you are really determined to hand in a dissertation you will need all the help that you can get, even if it is hard to take.

Once you have arranged an appointment with your supervisor (don't just turn up, even though time is tight) spend a few minutes reading the rest of this chapter. Go to the meeting with a plan, even if it's only an outline of how you think it might be possible. This shows that you are serious about finishing the dissertation and that you do care. Importantly, it shows that you're not expecting your supervisor to tell you what to do. You'll need their help to figure out what's feasible in the time you have left, but ultimately it's you who needs to produce the work.

If you no longer have a supervisor

It is possible that if you haven't done any work towards your dissertation that the person assigned to supervise you is no longer able to help you. However, you will need to find someone to help you as you are going to need help to work out what's feasible and what is expected of you. At this point, I would seek out the help of another member of academic staff, but again, don't expect to find someone at such short notice. Asking a friend or relative to help would be the next step, ideally someone who has written a dissertation before.

I cannot emphasise strongly enough that this is not a situation you want to be in.

Stop . . .

So, you have completed your data collection/analysis and you have just a few days left, but there still seems a lot to get through.

Don't panic, take a break

Towards the end of the dissertation it can seem like there is still a huge amount to do and not enough time to complete it in.

It might feel strange, but you need to take a break from your dissertation. Taking a break can give you a little bit of distance, so that when you come back to it you can be rational and objective. Snooze for 15 minutes, bake a cake, go for a short run; it just needs to be a short break. When you start afresh, skip ahead to 'Form a timetable'.

Finish collecting data and start writing

Sometimes, people run out of time to write up because they don't have a fixed end point in their data collection. There comes a point when you *must* stop collecting data and just get writing, because otherwise you will run out of time. It is very easy to carry on with the data collection; because once you're underway it's a task that you are familiar with and it becomes easy to do. Starting something new is always hard and writing up is always a new experience, even if you've done it before. Don't let the intimidation stop you from doing it. Read the previous section, take a break and then we'll tackle the next stage.

Form a timetable

Once you've had a chance to step back from the dissertation, sit down and plan out what you still have to do and when you plan to do it. When you create a final plan work backwards and make sure you do it in pencil, you will probably have to juggle things a little to fit them all into the time you have left. When you submit your dissertation it is best to have a project that is finished, rather than one that's incomplete, so plan your time to make sure you tackle *every* section, including all the front and end sections required, even if you can't do them to the level you wanted to.

What's finished and what's still to do?

Before you can plan your time between now and your deadline, you need to know where you are at the moment. Make a list or a table, like the one overleaf, to summarise what's finished, what's part way through and what is yet to be started.

Chapter	Complete?	What's still to do?
Introduction	No	Rewrite after I've finished everything else.
Literary Review	Almost	Proofread.
Methodology	Yes	
Results	Almost	Proofread.
Interpretation	No	Still need to finish writing.
Conclusion	No	Not started.
Start and end sections	No	Some are partly started, like the bibliography.

'Plan your work so that the majority of it falls into your productive times.'

Work backwards from your hand-in date

Make sure you read chapter 9 and fully understand what needs to happen at the end of the writing process, from front and end sections, to printing and binding. Once you have allowed time for this, work backwards through proofreading, redrafting and writing, giving a realistic amount of time for everything. It might not be as much time as you would like, but make sure everything is included,

Know when you work best

There will be points in the day when you are not as productive as others. I find I work best in the morning and the evening. Afternoons are often a waste of time for me. Plan your work so that the majority of it falls into your productive times. Use your unproductive times for any other essential jobs, such as if you have a job interview or need to collect children from school. Also, be prepared to use your unproductive time productively, there is nothing like the threat of an upcoming deadline to make you work throughout the day into the night.

Leave time for proofreading

The advice from Dr Emma Waterton, Senior Lecturer in Social Sciences at the University of Western Sydney, is 'proofread your work prior to submission do not just write the final sentence and then hit "print".'

Even if it feels like you don't have time to finish writing, make sure that you or someone else proofreads your work. So much work is spoilt by lack of proofreading. See chapter 9 for more proofreading tips.

Set yourself targets

Set yourself measurable targets within a specific time, e.g. '1,000 words today' or 'complete methodology before lunch'. With only a limited amount of time, you will have to stick to these targets and move on to the next task at the time you have allotted. You will know how you work best, but you could always build in some extra time at the end of the day to finish off any of the tasks that might have overrun.

Prepare for a prolonged period at your desk

You will be at your desk for a lot of time over the next couple of weeks. Spend a few minutes thinking about what you'll need. Don't use going shopping every day as an excuse to stop writing – at this point you need all the time you can get.

Avoid distractions

There is nothing worse than finally sitting down to write and something happens to distract you. I spent some of my time writing my PhD in a large shared work space; I remember chatting to a friend one day and asking what she was listening to on the headphones she always wore. She smiled and said, 'Nothing. If I wear headphones people don't disturb me, they think I'm listening to something.'

How to avoid distractions:

- Put an answerphone message on your mobile saying that you'll reply to calls at a certain time. Then switch it to airplane mode and only check for messages during breaks.
- Wear headphones.
- Rearrange all unimportant appointments, e.g. haircuts.
- Deal with anything that's nagging at you before you start work, rather than part way through the day.
- If there are too many distractions at home/the library, try a new place to work.

Turn yourself off to the (online) world

'Email and social network sites are great for keeping in touch with people. But they are also a huge distraction.'

Email and social network sites are great for keeping in touch with people. But they are also a huge distraction. I usually work with them open in a separate window, so I have to choose when to look at them, rather than stumble across a friend's status while I'm trying to do research online. However, there comes a point when the deadline needs to take priority. At this point, emails and social networks are completely banished, unless I'm on a break. At this late stage, find a way to manage your online life, so that it doesn't distract you:

- Turn off pop-up notifications.
- Switch off the Wi-Fi.

Food

Make sure you eat regularly and try to eat as healthily as you can. With limited time there is a real temptation to turn to junk food because it's quick, easy and satisfies cravings. It can also leave you feeling lethargic, which isn't good when you want to be alert and writing. See chapter 8 for a list of foods that are good for you, and importantly, good for your brain.

Drink

Similar to food, drinks can seriously affect your performance. If you need to get yourself going the temptation is to turn to tea and coffee for a caffeine fix. If you find yourself drinking a lot of caffeinated drinks, try to reduce them, cut them out altogether or vary them with other drinks. The best thing to drink is just water, but you might find that unappealing if it's cold, so something like a glass of hot fruit cordial or squash is warming, refreshing and helps to keep you hydrated.

Support

Throughout most of the book I have suggested that the first port of call for help should be your supervisor. This is still the case with technical details, but in the last few weeks or days, it will normally be your friends and family who offer you the most support.

Supervisor

Your supervisor isn't there to help motivate you in the last few days or weeks. If you have any last-minute problems with data or interpretation, you should certainly contact them, but at this stage it's about you finishing the dissertation, not about them helping you. Your contact with your supervisor will be all but over; they should have read the last draft chapters and your meetings will have finished. If you have arranged for them to read any more of your work, perhaps a last chapter or to look over some corrections, make sure you continue to stick to your deadline for them even though you'll be trying to complete other chapters.

Friends and family

Just because your contact time with your supervisor is almost over, that doesn't mean that you can't find support from other people. In fact, it is likely to be the support of people close to you that makes a huge difference in getting the dissertation finished on time.

Friends and family are likely to want to help you, especially if you are getting stressed by the lack of time. There are lots of ways they can make your life easier in the last couple of weeks/days:

- Ask them to do some of the cooking/shopping/cleaning that you might normally do (you'll find out if they really want to help you when you ask this one!).

- Ask them to proofread finished chapters. It is hard to spot your own mistakes, so another pair of eyes can be useful.

- If you need to get multiple copies bound before submitting, ask if they can give you a lift to the binders.

- They can provide a useful distraction when you take a break. Ask what's been going on for them; you'll soon get caught up in someone else's life, giving you a much earned break – just make sure you get back to work when you'd planned to.

- If you have friends who are also writing a dissertation, don't be afraid to talk to them and share problems. There is a high possibility that they are experiencing similar problems to you. It might even be worth arranging to meet up every few days to compare notes. Knowing that you aren't the only one finding it hard can make it easier.

- Friends and family can also help to keep you on track. If you know that you are not good at managing your time, give them a copy of your work plan and ask them to help to keep you on track. Just knowing that someone else knows what you should be doing can be a good motivational tool.

Friends and family are vital in the last few days, but equally, you need to make sure that they give you the peace and quiet that you need to finish the dissertation. If you think they are likely to distract you, try to explain to them that for the next few days you really need to concentrate on finishing the dissertation. You could always arrange to do something special with them after you have finished, which will make them feel wanted and will give you both something to look forward to.

'Friends and family are likely to want to help you, especially if you are getting stressed by the lack of time.'

Employers and colleagues

If you work part-time alongside studying, you will probably need to take time off in the last week. Think about this in advance and book the time off. If you can't take holiday, or need extra time off, talk to your employer. If you sit down and explain the situation, they will more than likely want to help you rather than risk losing a valued employee or risk making you ill (so you wouldn't be able to work anyway). You could always offer to work extra time after you have finished the dissertation. The more you offer them, the harder it is for them to refuse.

You might also find a similar level of support from colleagues as you would from close friends and family. Sometimes, friends will be struggling with the same problems and your family might be far away or people might be so busy that they can't offer you much support. In these instances, it will often be work colleagues who have been through the same situation as you that can offer you the most support. Take any help they offer, especially in the latter stages, like proofreading, checking your bibliography or checking your figures.

Summing Up

- If you haven't started your dissertation and you only have a few weeks before you need to submit, you need to find help from a supervisor, another member of academic staff or someone who understands what is involved in writing a dissertation. These people will be able to help you work out what is feasible. Avoid getting into this situation at all costs.

- At the end of the dissertation there is a temptation to panic because there seems a lot to do in a short space of time. Try not to stress. Assess what you still have to do and plan your time so that you can tackle each element.

- In the last few days you need to avoid as many distractions as possible. Switch off email notifications, ask friends or family to do your share of the shopping/house work and arrange time off work.

- Use your friends, family and colleagues for support in the last few days. They can help with proofreading, feeding you or just giving you moral support.

Glossary

Aims

Aims are what you are wanting to achieve in your dissertation.

Bibliography

A list of all the sources that you have cited in your dissertation. It can also contain all the other sources that you have read but not cited.

Citation

This is the reference to the source that has provided the information you have just summarised or quoted.

Descriptive statistics

Statistics that help you to describe your data.

Dissertation

A substantial piece of original and individual research that is written as part of an undergraduate degree programme. It is usually about 10,000 words long and is written in the second or third year.

E-book

A book that has been digitised and can be read on a computer or downloaded to other devices.

Figures

A picture, illustration, photo, diagram or image in a dissertation.

Gant chart

A type of chart that you can use to help you plan your dissertation. It plots the tasks against time.

Grade descriptors

A set of criteria for each grade bracket. They are especially useful if you are aiming to get a particular grade.

Metadata

Is often described as data about data. For example, if you take a photograph (data) the metadata is the image number, the details of the camera it was taken on, the date and time the photo was taken.

Objective (adjective)

To take a factual or balanced view of a subject. To be unprejudiced by personal opinion. The opposite of 'subjective'.

Objectives (noun)

Are how you are going to achieve your aims.

Paraphrase

Putting someone else's ideas in your own words.

Plagiarism

When another person's work or ideas are portrayed as your own.

Reference list

A list of all the sources cited in a dissertation.

Signposting

Using headings, structure and particular words to indicate to the reader what's coming next.

Social sciences

A group of academic subjects that study human nature and society. They include: anthropology, archaeology, criminology, economics, education, linguistics, law, communication studies, history, political science, sociology, human geography and psychology.

Subjective

A personal perspective, therefore it is likely to be one side of a wider argument or biased. The opposite of 'objective'.

Supervisor

Someone who can offer you advice and guidance during the dissertation process.

Table

Data that is organised into columns and rows. A spreadsheet is often presented as a table.

Tense

A grammatical term that tells you when something happened.

Appendix

Appendix 1 – Aims and Objectives

The following is an extract from a first class undergraduate dissertation in geography, by Robin Wilson:

Title: Automated Selection of Suitable Atmospheric Calibration Sites for Satellite Imagery

The aim of this project is:

To develop an automated system to identify suitable targets for atmospheric correction of medium and high resolution satellite imagery.

Three objectives have been formulated, although it should be noted that successful completion of these objectives does not necessarily mean successful fulfilment of the aim:

1. To develop a set of criteria which can be used to select calibration sites for atmospheric correction.

2. To implement an automatic site selection routine based on these criteria using ENVI/IDL and eCognition.

3. To assess the quality of the calibration site selection both qualitatively and quantitatively.

Help List

Helplines/Support

Mind Your Head Oxford

http://mindyourheadoxford.wordpress.com/

A website run by Oxford University Student Union about their mental health awareness campaign. Includes links to other online resources.

Nightline

www.nightline.ac.uk

Use the website to find your local nightline. Nightline provides emotional support to students in distress from academic stress, bullying or debt, to loneliness, depression or bereavement; from arguments with flatmates or worries about a friend to addictions, eating disorders or self-harm; from relationship or family problems to sexuality, sexual abuse or abortion.

Student organisations

NUS (National Union of Students)

www.nus.org.uk

NUS HQ, Macadam House, 275 Gray's Inn Road, London WC1X 8QB

Tel: 0845 5210 262

The NUS promotes, defends and extends the rights of students and develops and champions strong students' unions. It also provides advice to students on its website.

NUS-USI (National Union of Students) Northern Ireland

http://www.nus.org.uk/en/nus-usi

42 Dublin Road, Belfast BT2 7HN

Tel: 028 9024 4641

info@nistudents.org

The NUS promotes, defends and extends the rights of students and develops and champions strong students' unions. It also provides advice to students on its website.

NUS (National Union of Students) Scotland

www.nus.org.uk/en/nus-scotland

1 Papermill Wynd, McDonald Road, Edinburgh, EH7 4QL

Tel: 0131 556 6598

mail@nus-scotland.org.uk

The NUS promotes, defends and extends the rights of students and develops and champions strong students' unions. It also provides advice to students on its website.

NUS-UCMC (National Union of Students) Wales

www.nus.org.uk/en/nus-wales

2nd floor, Cambrian Buildings, Mount Stuart Square, Cardiff CF10 5FL

UCMC, 2il Lawr, Adeiladau Cambrian, Sgwâr Mount Stuart, Caerdydd, CF10 5FL

Tel: 02920 435 390

office@nus-wales.org.uk

The NUS promotes, defends and extends the rights of students and develops and champions strong students' unions. It also provides advice to students on its website.

Planning and researching your dissertation

Aims and objectives:

http://www.hollings.mmu.ac.uk/index.php?option=com_content&task=view&id=45&Itemid=140

This website provides in-depth information about how to write the aims and objectives of your dissertation.

General information on Dissertations:

http://learn.solent.ac.uk/mod/book/view.php?id=4628&chapterid=11573

This is a very good dissertation handbook from Southampton Solent University. It is especially useful for writing dissertation proposals and for understanding the requirements of each chapter.

Interpreting your results

UsableStats

http://www.usablestats.com

This website has some good introductory tutorials about statistics.

Writing your dissertation

Grammar and writing advice

http://learnhigher.ac.uk/Students/Academic-Writing.html

This website has a series of useful guides and quizzes to help you with academic writing.

Signposting words

Peter Redman and Wendy Maples's book *Good Essay Writing: A Social Sciences Guide* has a good section on linking words. This section is also available online at: http://www.sagepub.com/redman/8.2.pdf. Have a look at them and try to apply them to your own writing.

Formatting your dissertation

Adding page numbers

This tutorial explains how to insert page numbers:

http://office.microsoft.com/en-gb/word-help/add-or-remove-headers-footers-and-page-numbers-HA010372690.aspx

Creating a list of figures/tables

This video takes you through how to create a list of figures:

http://www.youtube.com/watch?v=G2RltLkC7vg

Using 'Captions'

This video takes you through using captions:

http://www.youtube.com/watch?v=khHQUg2CVGw

Working with 'Styles'

This video shows you how to use and edit Styles in your dissertation:

http://www.youtube.com/watch?v=Gq_dr69xjTw

Keeping Healthy

Food for Health: The Essential Guide

http://need2knowbooks.co.uk/food-for-health-essential-guide.

By Sara Kirkham (2010), Need2Know Publishing.

A good book for advice on how to achieve a healthy, nutritious diet without breaking the bank, including useful meal plans for a range of health conditions and specific information on how to improve your memory.

NHS choices – Healthy eating

www.nhs.uk/livewell/healthy-eating/

The healthy eating section of the National Health Service website provides tips on what to eat and what to avoid in order to stay healthy. There are also sections on health issues that are particularly related to students.

Vitamin C

http://extrahappiness.com/happiness/?p=4415

This website has more information on vitamin C and why it is good for you.

WedMD

www.webmd.com

WebMD provides valuable health information, tools for managing your health, and support to those who seek information.

Book List

Food for Health: The Essential Guide, by Sara Kirkham, Need2Know, 2010. £9.99.

Good Essay Writing A Social Sciences Guide, by Peter Redman and Wendy Maples, The Open University, 2011. £13.99.

The Good Study Guide, by Andrew Northedge, The Open University, 2005. £12.99. This is a great book for learning how to study. This I something that gets taken for granted once you know how, but, like driving, it's entirely puzzling when you begin.

Your Undergraduate Dissertation: The Essential Guide for Success, by Nicholas S R Walliman, SAGE, 2004. £15.99. Most of the book is also available as a free e-book at: http://books.google.co.uk/books/about/Your_Undergraduate_Dissertation.html?id=B-U0FfMDMq0C

References

Akister, J, Williams, I and Maynard A, 'Group Supervision of Undergraduate Dissertations: A preliminary enquiry into student experiences and outcomes', Practice and Evidence of the Scholarship of teaching and Learning in Higher Education, 2009, vol. 4, issue 3, 77-94.

BBC Good Food [Online] '10 foods to boost your brainpower', http://www.bbcgoodfood.com/content/wellbeing/features/boost-brainpower/1/, (accessed 13 April 2013.)

Department of Health http://www.nhs.uk/Livewell/Goodfood/Pages/eight-tips-healthy-eating.aspx, accessed 13 April 2013.)

Harvard University [Online] 'Notes on skimming a book or reading selectively', isites.harvard.edu/fs/docs/icb...files/tips_on_skimming.doc, (accessed 17 April 2013).

Health and Safety Executive [Online] 'Working with VDUs', http://www.hse.gov.uk/pubns/indg36.pdf, (accessed 12 April 2013).

Hudson, R and Walmsley, J, 'The English Patient: English grammar and teaching in the twentieth century', Journal of Linguistics, 2005, vol. 41, issue 3, http://www.phon.ucl.ac.uk/home/dick/papers/texts/engpat.pdf, (accessed 22 April 2013).

Kay, B and Maclean, C Knee deep in claret. 1985, Auld Alliance Publishing.

Korkki, P [Online] 'To Stay on Schedule, Take a Break', The New York Times, 16 June 2012, http://nyti.ms/LcUmnU, (accessed 12 April 2013).

LearnHigher [Online] 'Academic Writing - Resources for Students', http://learnhigher.ac.uk/Students/Academic-Writing.html (accessed 10 April 2013).

NHS Choices [Online] 'Eight tips for healthy living', www.nhs.uk/Livewell/Goodfood/Pages/eight-tips-healthy-eating.aspx, (accessed 13 April 2013.)

NHS Choices [Online] 'Coping with stress', www.nhs.uk/Livewell/studenthealth/Pages/Copingwithstress.aspx, (accessed 13 April 2013).

Mondofacto [Online] 'Writing a Discussion', http://www.mondofacto.com/study-skills/research/how-to-write-your dissertation/05.html, (accessed 3 May 2013).

Morley, J, [Online] 'Academic Phrasebank', http://www.phrasebank.manchester.ac.uk/, (accessed 20 April 2013).

Rampen, J [Online] 'Brits feel more productive after holidays', Workplace Savings and Benefits, 18 June 2012, http://www.wsandb.co.uk/wsb/news/2185003/brits-feel-productive-holidays, (accessed 12 April 2013).

Redman, P and Maples, W, 'Great Signposting Words', in Good Essay Writing A Social Sciences Guide, 2011, The Open University. http://www.sagepub.com/redman/8.2.pdf, (accessed 19 April 2013).

The Higher Education Statistics Agency. [Online] 'Statistics - Students and qualifiers at UK HE institutions', http://www.hesa.ac.uk/content/view/1897/239/ (accessed 8 February 2013).

The University of York. [Online] 'Mature Students', http://www.york.ac.uk/study/undergraduate/applying/mature, (accessed 10 February 2013).

Useable Stats [Online] 'Fundamentals of Statistics 1: Basic Concepts Tutorial', http://www.usablestats.com/tutorials/basicStats, (accessed 2 May 2013).

Vasagar, J [Online] 'Number of UK university applicants drops 8.7%, Ucas figures show', The Guardian, 30 January 2012, http://www.guardian.co.uk/education/2012/jan/30/uk-university-applications-drop-ucas, (accessed 9 February 2013).

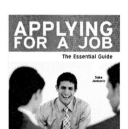
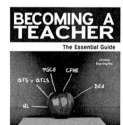